Nevis Travel and Tourism, Caribbean.

Touristic Guide

Author
Wyatt Harris

Published
By
Information-Source.
16192 Coastal Highway Lewes,
DE 19958. USA

Table of Content

Nevis Guide, Caribbean

Introduction

A quiet, unspoiled island located in the former British Leeward Islands of the northern Caribbean, Nevis is two miles south of St. Kitts, 60 miles west of Antigua, 70 miles south of St. Maarten and 200 miles south of Puerto Rico. The island is dominated by a central mountain rising to 3,232 feet. From the cloud-covered peak, lush slopes fall to coral and volcanic sand beaches below. The island has a population of about 9,000 people and is approximately 6 miles by 8 miles in size. An almost round island, set like a gem in the tropical seas; some call Nevis the Jewel of the Caribbean.

Nevis is a really great "get-away-from-it-all" destination: there are no chain restaurants on Nevis, no casinos, no billboards, no nightclubs, almost no "serious" shopping, and no traffic lights. Nevis is very quiet, very natural, and very beautiful. You will not find hawkers pestering you on the beach; the taxi drivers will not pester you for a fare as you walk along the road; Nevis people are dignified. They can be a little bit shy at first, but they are very kind once they know who you are. Nevis is developed enough to be convenient and pleasant, but not developed enough to be spoiled.There are very few places left in the Caribbean that are like Nevis!

Contextual

Nevis History

Nevis was first settled about 2000 years ago by Amerinidians who travelled north from what is now Venezuela. Many centuries later Columbus saw the island and gave it a name, but he did not set foot on it. Colonial settlement on Nevis began with the British in the early 1600s.

Nevis rapidly became the center of the British Caribbean sugar trade and slave trade. The island produced exceptionally large amounts of sugar on its numerous sugar cane plantations, and became known as "The Queen of the Caribbees". The Bath Hotel just to the south of the capital was a spa hotel built in 1778 next to the Bath hot spring. This appears to have been the very first tourist hotel in the Caribbean.

Horatio Nelson was stationed on the island for a while when he was a young naval officer, and during that time he met Frances Nisbet, who he married in 1787. American founding father, Alexander Hamilton was born on Nevis in 1789, and lived on the island until he was eight. There are local museums honoring both of these gentlemen.

A history of Nevis, which can be ordered over the web or bought on the island is Swords, Ships, and Sugar by *Vince Hubbard* . The author, who still resides on Nevis, writes in a lively style, and has managed to unearth many entertaining stories from Nevis' past.

Many architectural ruins of old sugar-plantation 'great houses', with their mills and associated buildings can be found scattered all over Nevis; some of these handsome old buildings have been converted into hotels, restaurants, dwellings, or remain as historic landmarks.

Nature

Interest in nature is on the rise, and for those who find joy in wild organisms of every kind, the tropics provide an unparalled opportunity to see nature at her most expressive and abundant. Nevis is an especially fine place for nature-lovers, because it is one of the few islands in the West Indies which is still relatively unspoiled, both on land and underwater.

Birdwatching is a lot of fun here: there are over 148 species that either live on the island year-round, or migrate through. A few birds are bright and showy, and several are rare or unusual. There are eight species of hawks, three different types of hummingbirds, and lots of different sea birds. To enjoy birding, try either hiking up the mountain in search of the Bridled Quail-dove and the elusive Purple-throated Carib (this is a hummingbird, not the beer!), or perhaps you would prefer to sit on the beach watching Magnificent Frigatebirds soar overhead like giant pterodactyls.

There are over 63 different kinds of butterflies on Nevis. Beautiful yellow ones are very common (these are several different kinds of Sulphur butterflies), but there are also orange, red, green, blue, white, and even black ones. All these can easily be found up the mountain, around gardens, or wherever there are lots of flowers. Butterflies are in fact Nevis's main natural pollinators, because honeybees are not native to the island.

Many of the birds, and all of the butterflies, flourish so well because of the rich plant life on Nevis. As far as introduced vegetation goes, there are hundreds of different kinds of palm trees, and thousands of beautiful flowering plants from all around the world (over 700 succulents alone). And of course, much of the original native plantlife of Nevis still exists, waiting to be properly documented; this ranges from giant trees hidden in valleys on the mountainside, to small delicate flowering plants on rocks by the shore.

Offshore, one can still find numerous types of coral, hundreds of species of crabs, brightly-coloured fish, and a bewildering variety of shell-bearing creatures. Living in some of the abandoned Queen Conch shells are small shrimps and the occasional small octopus. Diving and snorkelling can really be a lot of fun on Nevis!

Architecture

This island was a very wealthy center for the sugar trade during the 17th, 18th, and 19th centuries, and as a result a lot of British colonial architecture was built, much of which still exists: some has been in continuous use, some has been restored, and some exists now only as picturesque ruins.

Dotted throughout the landscape of Nevis there are countless pieces of functional architecture from sugar processing, (conical sugar mills, boiling houses, etc) as well as quite a lot of domestic architecture, including elegant plantation "great houses".

Charlestown, the capital, has several impressive stone buildings from the 18th and early 19th centuries, including the library and courthouse building, and the Bath Hotel. In the town there are also a lot of attractive 19th century buildings with traditional gingerbread trim.

Many of the older churches on Nevis are handsome, well-proportioned structures, built using cut volcanic stone, and having open-air windows and storm shutters. These buildings were very well-designed for their situation, and some have proved strong enough to withstand both hurricanes and seismic activity.

At every one of the Nevis Plantation Inns, well-preserved buildings from the historic past are in use. You can chose to simply pass by and look at these buildings, or perhaps you would prefer to stay a little longer and have afternoon tea, eat dinner, or stay in: Nisbet, Old Manor, Golden Rock and Montpelier.

The oldest building is at The Hermitage where the 360 year-old great house is one of the oldest wooden residences still standing in the Caribbean.

Although many local Nevisian people now live in modern, concrete-block houses, there are also still many examples on the island of the local vernacular wooden cottages, which are constructed in modular style, and which can be moved from one place to another. These interesting small Caribbean cottages are referred to as "Chattel Houses."

Those looking for adventure and willing to hike might like to visit some of the ruins hidden up the mountain. There are underground rooms, three-story remains, and old bridges found everywhere, dating from when Nevis was truly the "Queen of the Caribbean".

Culture

After 2,000 years of colonization by Amerindians, Nevis was settled in the early 1600's by the British.

The island rapidly became an important center for sugar farming, and even though no sugar cane is grown commercially on Nevis now, the island still has a primarily agrarian feel and culture. This means that sometimes Nevisians may not seem as "polished" as people might appear to be in some other destinations, but the small farming that still exists here certainly means that the produce on Nevis is excellent, but it also means that on this island you will meet kind, honest, straightforward people, who are dignified and polite. Some may be shy, but they are friendly and kind beneath that shyness, and they are uncorrupted by the perils of big-city living. The literacy rate on Nevis, by the way, is one of the highest in the world.

The people of Nevis are very religious: the island has over 53 churchs, and Christmas and Easter are big holidays here, which are celebrated with not only the expected things, such as traditional Christmas lights, but also with horse racing and kite contests.

Health and Safety

You don't need any special shots in order to come to Nevis, and things like salads and fresh fruit, tap water and local ice-cream are all perfectly safe, as well as being delicious!

The incidence of crime on Nevis by most people's standards is very low indeed, but it does occasionally happen, so it's worth taking sensible precautions.

There are no large predatory animals on the island, so you also don't need to worry about about lions, tigers or even Tyrannosaurs!

Most hotels and rental homes have safes, so please lock up those beautiful earrings, especially when you are out snorkeling or diving. Why? Because sparkling things attract small fish, which may then want to nibble on your earlobes!

However, all that being said, there are some comments that need to be made. Nevis doesn't want any accidents to happen to visitors, so:

Do not sit under coconut trees, because of the danger of falling nuts! This sounds like a joke, but it really is a serious point: a coconut (complete with its very heavy green husk) dropping from the top of a tree can be a lethal missile.

If you want to go hiking, please go with a guide, or tell someone exactly where you are going, and when you will be back. If a rock falls on you while climbing up that ruin for a better view, and you need some help getting back, it is a great advantage if someone knows where you are.

Stay away from babies, because mothers can be fierce about protecting their young, whether it's mother donkeys, mother pigs, or even the mothers of those attractive teenage girls!

Drive on the correct side of the road. Nevis still drives British style, which means on the left of the road.

If you do encounter a problem, please let either your hotel know or call the police, both are there to help.

Here are some additional, more minor items:

Do be careful not to get badly sunburned, especially during the first few days you are in the tropics. You may feel plenty cool enough, because of the breeze and the pleasant temperature of the seawater, but in the tropics the UV rays during the midday hours are fierce, especially when your skin is not used to it. Use plenty of sunblock and enjoy some relaxing shade some of the time. A man's long-sleeve shirt made of thin cotton makes an easy and pleasant cover-up for beach or for snorkeling.

Most hotels provide bug repellent sprays, because if you are near the beach, in the hour or two around sunset you may find that tiny sand flies become active and bite, especially if the breeze has dropped. Mosquitos may also be encountered, but they are usually not much of a problem in most areas on Nevis.

If you are going to do a lot of exploring without a guide in wild places and on waste ground, ask someone to show you how to recognize the small heap of fine earth that marks a nest of fire ants, so that you can avoid treading on those. Also ask to be shown what horse nettles look like, so that you can avoid touching them.

Neighborhoods

Nevis has Caribbean villages rather than neighborhoods, and most of them are quiet and peaceful rather than bustling: people take things easy on this little island in the West Indies.

There is Charlestown, the capital of Nevis: if you walk really slowly it can take almost 20 minutes to go from one side of town to the other. Of course, stopping for shopping and a drink, this may take longer. And if you drink a lot, it could take hours! Charlestown has the feel of the Old Caribbean. Its architecture has not changed much since the 1800's. The main buildings are stone with the back "tracks" still having wooden houses with the occasional "Gingerbread Trim".

On the rest of the island you will find over 25 small villages and communities. Each one has a shop and a church (some have several churchs) and you are welcome to stop at either. Butler's Village on the Atlantic coast was reportedly where Jimmy Buffet played dominos at "Butler's Domino College" and Barnes Ghaut is a really nice village, up on the mountainside above Four Seasons.

Please be careful when driving through villages. Watch for children playing cricket in the streets and for livestock: mainly chickens, sheep, and goats, (the cows and donkeys will look after themselves.)

Weather and When to Go

Yes, Nevis is in the tropics, but it is a small island cooled by almost constant breezes off of the ocean, so it never gets really hot. The weather also doesn't change much all year round on Nevis, except during hurricanes, which are infrequent (the last one to really affect Nevis was Lenny, 1999, and there was a brush with Omar in 2008).

The Atlantic side of the island has stronger breezes than the Caribbean side, and the higher up the mountain you are, the cooler the temperature is, and the stronger the breeze is too. When you are high up, you are more likely to get evening or early-morning showers, as clouds usually form around the peak of the central mountain, Nevis Peak, especially at night.

The winter temperature averages 79º F (26.1º C), with daily ranges from a low of 75º F up to a high of 85º F. Wind speed is usually about 10 15 mph, but can get higher during December for a few days, as the winter solstice passes. Winter is the ideal time for people to escape the frigid north and enjoy the lovely warm seas around Nevis.

The summer temperatures on Nevis are also good, being only 3º F higher than the winter, averaging 82º F (27.8º C). Winds are usually less strong in the summertime, except of course during tropical storms or hurricanes. Because there is less wind, the ocean water is calmer and slightly warmer, so summer is ideal for diving. And because the climate on Nevis never gets very hot or very humid, summer is also a good time for people from the southern parts of the USA to leave behind all that stifling heat and humidity. Nevis beaches are never crowded, and both airline rates and hotel rates are cheaper in the summer.

In terms of what to wear, shorts and thin tee-shirts are OK for outdoors. But this is the tropics, so if you prefer to be cooler still, bring loose-fitting, woven (not knitted) clothing, made of light-weight cotton cloth, or better yet, thin linen cloth. Linen shirts and dresses are the coolest of all because they allow the breeze to blow right through. A suitable sun hat of some sort with a brim is an excellent idea, and don't forget to bring your sunglasses, and lots of high SPF sunblock. Skin used to more northern climes can burn very quickly indeed in the tropics, and a tropical sunburn can be quite painful, so be careful with this, especially if you are outside in the middle of the day. Whether you are male or female, a man's long-sleeved thin cotton shirt makes an easy and comfortable cover-up for beach or snorkeling.

An umbrella is generally not needed, although you may encounter the occasional shower, more so in summer than in winter. If you are sensitive to cooling off, and are staying on the Atlantic coast (which is windy) or up around 1,000 feet (which is much cooler), then you may find that a shirt with long sleeves is more comfortable in the evenings.

If you are going to be staying at one of the elegant, upscale hotels, then in order to be dressed appropriately for dinner, men need to bring a pair of long pants (not jeans, not shorts) and a couple of shirts other than tee-shirts (no tie or jacket is needed, and Hawaiian shirts are just fine.) Covered shoes rather than flip-flops are also part of the dress code for men. For dinnertime at the upscale hotels women need to bring a dress, or a nice skirt and blouse, or nice-looking pants. No shorts or jeans at dinner, and no tee-shirts. There is a strong tradition of dressing up a little in the evening at the fancier hotels, and with the oil lamps burning, the stars twinkling, and the soft tropical breeze blowing, it all makes a for an elegant, old-fashioned Caribbean evening.

Historical and Conservation Society

The Nevis Historical and Conservation Society (NHCS) is a well-respected nonprofit organisation, which was founded in 1980, and is devoted to conserving the nature, culture, and history of the island of Nevis.

The society created both the Alexander Hamilton Museum and the Horatio Nelson Museum, and is active on many different fronts, including organizing numerous events and publishing a newsletter called 'The Gathering', which comes out twice yearly.

The NHCS, together with the University of Southhampton, England, and the Bristol and Region Archeology Service, England, are responsible for the brightly-colored, well-designed and well-written 'Nevis Heritage Trail' signs that you will see in many interesting areas all over the island.

For a nominal sum, those who are interested in helping the island protect its natural, historical and cultural riches, can support the NHCS by becoming a member. The headquarters of NHCS is at the Museum of Nevis History in Charlestown, Nevis.

Archeology

Nevis, one of the first British colonies in the Caribbean, is very rich in archeological interest.

Teams of archeologists from the U.S. and Britain have, during recent years, examined many prehistoric and historic sites on Nevis, ranging from 2,000 year old settlements to 19th century plantations. Some of this work was featured in a well-received, two-part BBC "Time Team" television program in 1998.

The first settlers on Nevis, 2,000 years ago, were Amerindians who traveled up from what is now Venezuela, colonizing the Lesser Antilles as they went. Nevis was an easy place to settle, because there was a good supply of freshwater, and rich intertidal areas where fish and conch were a steady source of food. So Nevis became home to a succession of prehistoric Amerindian cultures, both pre-ceramic and ceramic, and they lived all around the island.

Budget Travel

Getting to Nevis is not difficult, and there are several different flight choices at different prices. The least expensive versions involve several flights and take many hours. if you are prepared to spend a little more, it is possible for example, to get a round trip non-stop flight to St. Kitts from New York via American Airlines, and then take a water taxi over to Nevis. Another possibility is an inexpensive Jet Blue flight to St.

Maarten, but the connecting flight from there to Nevis is not cheap. However once you are on Nevis, there is quite a wide variety of small guest houses, which are well-equipped and inexpensive.

The guest houses are scattered in various places around the island. There are Specialty Lodging and Guest Houses, or best of all you can ask the Nevis Tourism Authority for help with choosing which guest house would best suit your particular needs. To email the NTA use: info@nevisisland.com

It is quite easy to travel around Nevis on a tight budget, because you can either use the inexpensive community buses (see the information in the listing about Public Transportation), or you can get lifts from people who are going your way. You simply wait at the side of the road and flag down vehicles by waving your hand in a downwards motion. When a bus driver sees this, he will stop for you unless the bus is already completely full of passengers, in which case the driver will flash his lights and drive on. Other people who are driving and who have room in their vehicle will often stop to give you a lift, and this is considered to be a perfectly respectable and traditional way to get around on Nevis.

Of course it is also possible to walk to many places you might need to go on Nevis, and this is usually quite pleasant, as long as it is not in the hottest part of the day. Renting a bicycle is another inexpensive option if you want to get around a lot according to your own schedule.

Inexpensive food should also not be a problem if you eat at local places (see the "Cheap Eats" article in the "Dining Scene" section of Traveler Articles for Nevis).

When leaving St. Kitts & Nevis to return to your home country, remember that there is an airport departure tax, an environmental levy and a small security charge to be paid, after checking in and before going through security. You can pay in local money or in dollars US. The total sum is about $22 US per person.

Communications

On vacation most of the time you want to be far away from your ordinary life back home, but international communication is necessary sometimes: for example, maybe you decide to stay a few days longer and the office needs to know. On Nevis, it's "No problem, man!"

There are several telephone providers which cellphone users can connect with, the roaming fees aren't bad (and after all, it's only for emergencies). Cable and Wireless are the longest established providers in the Caribbean and they also handle T-Mobile. Recently AT&T through Cingular have started service to Nevis. There is a Digicel company right in Charlestown.

Internet connections can be found at all the hotels, and WiFi is also becoming more and more common around the island.

Explaining Nevis

Two topics that have been raised in reviews are the color of the beach sand, and prices in general on Nevis. It seems that some reviewers did not know what to expect, or drew the wrong conclusions. There is also some misinformation out there.

None of the beaches on Nevis are white sand, because white sand is formed solely from coral, and so it is generally found only on flat coral islands, such as the Bahamas or Anguilla. The sand on Nevis is instead formed from the natural volcanic rock of the island, and as a result, most Nevis beaches have attractive pale yellow sand, or slightly greyish-yellow sand.

The high iron content of the volcanic rock means that some of the beaches on the southern and eastern coasts of Nevis have dark reddish-grey sand, or even black sand. (Local children sometimes have fun by dragging a magnet along this kind of beach in order to watch the magnet get "furry" with iron particles!)

One vision-impaired visitor commented that Nevis sand is a lot smoother than other places he had visited, and he said the sand felt hotter. This is because the darker colour absorbs the heat better, and this actually is really great for the nesting Sea Turtles which visit the island. The volcanic nutrients and iron also increase life on both land and sea, and so the waters around Nevis may not always be quite as intense a blue as in some other flatter places, but to make up for that, Nevis does have a beautiful big green mountain with interesting rain forest to visit!

The price of items for sale on the island is another subject that a few people have mentioned: one reviewer imagined that there was "an 80% tax", but this is most certainly not the case, although it is true that prices can be high. The businesses on Nevis try to import the best things they can, at the most reasonable prices, but Nevis is a "terminal destination" for shipping, such that almost all items have to be shipped in, with very little at all going out, and this very much adds to the overall cost. And because Nevis is only a small island, the local businesses generally cannot get the cheap rates associated with big, discount places. It is also worth remembering that goods shipped to Nevis from the U.S. have to pass through at least three ports (Miami, San Juan, St. Kitts) and in some cases up to five ports. Each port charges taxes and fees, which are usually around 10–15% per stop; and then once the merchandize arrives on Nevis, the business which sells the item has to cover their own costs too.

So why go to Nevis? Because, while the beaches are not pure white, they are very lovely; and the shallow sea, where you swim and snorkel, is not "dead" as so many others elsewhere are; this is the living Caribbean. Look for the hidden beaches, where the turtles nest and eat turtle grass off-shore, where the tiny octopus makes his home inside the empty Queen Conch shell, and where the tropic birds soar overhead. The beautiful green mountain on Nevis has dense rain forest, which you won't find any trace of on a flat coral island, and the high slopes generate more breeze to keep you cooler. Prices may be high, but you will find friendly, dignified people, and your satisfaction will be as great or greater still than the price you pay to discover it.

Nevis is a safe, healthy, and relaxing destination, very beautiful and with a lot to see.

Guest Houses

Although the island of Nevis is generally considered to be a high-end destination, the Caribbean also has a tradition of inexpensive Guest Houses, and Nevis has quite a few of them. It is certainly possible to find a nice place to stay on Nevis without paying high prices for a fancy hotel or resort.

A Guest House is like a simple version of a hotel or rooming house, and Nevis has a number of them in various different locations all over the island: some are near the coast, some are further inland. Some are in Charlestown the capital, and some are in the countryside. Some are next to the main road, some are set back some distance from a road. They mostly offer modest but pleasant accommodations at bargain prices.

The cost of a room varies a great deal from one Guest House to the next. The overall range is from US $35 a night for a simple room, to as high as US $ 130 a night for a 3-bedroom apartment with full kitchen, in the low season. Most of the accomodations are in the $50 to $80 range.

Each Guest House offers a different range of amenities, so check what is offered before booking. Most rooms have air conditioning and television, some have phones and en-suite bathrooms. Some rooms in some Guest Houses have a full kitchen and a living room. Some Guest Houses have their own restaurant. The Guest Houses usually do not spend much money on advertising, and therefore many of them don't really have much of an on-line presence.

Some of the Nevis Guest Houses are as follows: in or near Charlestown: Philsha's Guest House, Sea Spawn, and JP's Guest House . Elsewhere on the island there are: The Five Star Guest House in

Gingerland, and The Ocean View Guest House in Newcastle. Some information on each one (except Cross Isles) can be found using a google search, and each one of the Guest Houses can be contacted via phone for more information.

If the Guest House is on or near the main road, it is possible to save even more money by not renting a car, and using the local buses instead.

As well as its Guest Houses, Nevis also has some mid-range options such as Bed and Breakfast places and small Inns.

Language and Etiquette

The language of Nevis is English, and basically it is the British variety. There is a strong local Caribbean accent, and there are also dialect words and dialect grammar which may be unfamiliar to visitors, however, local people who talk regularly with tourists always try to make sure that they are easy to understand.

When saying hello to people that you don't know, it is more polite to use the English forms: "Good morning", "Good afternoon", "Good evening" and so on, rather than the American, "Hi!". Nevisians in general tend to be very polite, and they are happy to meet other people who also have good manners.

Nevis culture has a strong religious foundation. Cursing in public is against the law. Nude bathing and topless bathing are not permitted. Beachwear is fine for the beach, but in public places it is not considered appropriate to be dressed in skimpy beach or resort clothes, such as short shorts or halter tops.

Please be sensitive to the fact that a lot of Nevisians are shy about being photographed. Please do not snap pictures of local people, their children, their homes or their personal property, without politely asking permission first.

Nevis is so very beautiful that even without disturbing people you will be able to go home with armfuls of lovely images.

Military History

This small Caribbean island has seen more than its fair share of battles, historically-speaking, because of its enormous wealth during the heyday of sugar.

Thanks to the sugar trade and the slave trade which went along with it, this one tiny island made more income for Britain during the 17th and early 18th centuries than all 13 colonies of

North America put together, despite the European demand for tobacco.

Over the years, the British colonial presence on Nevis was called upon to fight the Dutch, the Spanish and the French, not to mention various fierce pirates with no particular national allegiance. Horatio Nelson was one of many promising young naval officers who spent time on Nevis.

A very fine history of Nevis, with particular emphasis on its military history, is "Swords, Ships and Sugar: History of Nevis"by Vincent K. Hubbard. The companion volume, "A History of St. Kitts: the Sweet Trade" is also excellent.

During the 17th and 18th centuries, fifteen fortifications were built on Nevis, although remains of only ten of them survive. A few of the sites were 'The Redoubt' in Newcastle: fortifications on Hurricane Hill and at Fort Ashby; also at 'Black Rocks' north of Charlestown; at Fort Charles south of Charlestown; and on Saddle Hill.

None of the surviving forts has been developed for tourism, and in some cases what remains of the fortification is minimal, but at Fort Charles, although grass and weeds have overgrown the site, some of the original cannons are still in position, overlooking Gallow's Bay and the Caribbean Sea.

Only in Nevis

Only in Nevis can you visit the birthplace and childhood home of Alexander Hamilton, overlooking the water. It's now a very good museum of the history and natural history of the island.

Only on Nevis can you eat dinner or have tea in the elegant plantation Great House where Horatio Nelson's wife Fanny, and her first husband's family (the Nisbets) used to live.

Only on Nevis can you stay on a lovely, green, almost round island, with a steep central volcanic mountain covered in rain forest, wreathed at the top in white clouds. The mountain makes a dramatic backdrop to almost every photograph you take, and the very attractive coastline of Nevis will probably also feature in almost every photograph you take.

Only on Nevis can you still see, and feel, and be in contact with, the wonderful old Caribbean as it used to be, back when Nevis was "Queen of the Caribbees", and yet still have the comfort and service of staying in well-equipped superb elegant hotels, either modern or historic.

Only on Nevis can you sit in complete safety and comfort, eating lunch surrounded in peace and nature, while watching volcanic activity taking place on nearby Montserrat.

Only on Nevis can you see wild monkeys on the golf course, turtles swimming right near town, chickens walking though an outdoor bar, goats eating someone's flower garden, ground lizards delighted to get a piece of french fry, fishermen selling multi-colored fish straight from the ocean, bananaquits and bullfinches stealing sugar from your breakfast bowl...

Only on Nevis on a clear day can you see three other Leeward Islands in one direction, and sometimes up to four other islands in another direction, including one small, steep and rocky, uninhabited island which was named by Columbus, which is only inhabited by goats, but which is now claimed as territory by more than four rival "Kings": one English, one American, one Italian, and one Spanish!

Only on Nevis can you be checking your e-mail one minute and then turn around and notice a beautiful small cannon from 1650 the next minute.

And, only on Nevis will you find so many visitors who have fallen in love with the place and keep coming back.

Places with Free Wifi

Oualie Beach Hotel, like most of the hotels on Nevis, has free wireless internet: you can sit in comfort at the bar and be connected to the internet. The private rental villa Veranda (www.nevisvillaholidays.com) has wireless internet. You can also get Wifi at the Medical University of the Americas, and several other places around the island.

The beaches on Nevis have Wifi in several places, including the area near Chevy's Calypso Bar & Grill on Pinneys Beach, a short distance south of the Four Seasons and immediately south of the Golden Rock Beach Pavilion. You can sit and enjoy a cocktail or lunch while surfing the web.

Telephone, Electricity, Water

Land-line telephone service on Nevis is really fairly good, but not quite perfect. If you are outside the country, the area code for Nevis is 869.

As of now, all of the land-line telephone numbers on the island have the same exchange: 469. This is convenient because if you are on Nevis and you are going to need to recall a number, all you need to memorize are the last 4 digits.

In addition, on Nevis there are three cellular telephone companies which have different numbers but the same area code. Many private homes as well as some hotels are now using those for guests rather than landlines because it give more flexibility and is less expensive. Their towers are discretely hidden around the island.

Ten years ago, the electrical power supply on Nevis was subject to not infrequent outages, but recently that has become a lot less common. Still, you may find that some parts of the island lose power, usually for short periods of time such as an hour or two, and this is not always due to equipment failure, it may in fact be due to planned repairs, but advance notice is not always given.

The basic power supply on Nevis is 230 volts and 60 cycles, however the hotels are wired for 110 volts, which is convenient for U.S. visitors. Some hotels also have European-type 220 volt outlets, but check with your hotel first if this is important to you.

The tap water on Nevis tastes very good, and is perfectly safe to drink, despite the current fashion for bottled water. Only those people who are extremely sensitive to water changes back home should feel that they should drink bottled water on Nevis.

Trivia and Fun Facts

Here are some cool snippets of information about this interesting Caribbean destination.

Nature Nevis has over 63 different species of butterflies, and over 140 species of birds, which are found all over the island. Some of the birds as well as some of the butterflies migrate over the sea - an interesting sight! There are also at least eight species of fascinating and harmless bats, many of which eat fruit or pollinate flowers. There are over 50 different varieties of mangoes here which fruit during the summer; all of the varieties are delicious, but each person has their own particular favourite.

History Nevis was at one time the highest-producing colony for sugar in the entire West Indies, and because of this, it was then known as the "Queen of the Caribbees", which means, the best of all the Caribbean islands. Alexander

Hamilton was born on Nevis, and Horatio Nelson got married here. Apparently he liked the "wedding package", which in his case was Frances 'Fanny' Nisbet, the widowed daughter-in-law of a Nevis plantation family, the Nisbets! You can still have dinner in Nisbet Plantation's great house, which was the Nisbet family's residence. Nevis also has the oldest library in the British Caribbean, and the oldest school for helping physically and mentally challenged children.

Transportation

Arriving and Departing

Nevis, West Indies, is a small Caribbean island. It has only one airport, which is quite elegant and modern, and big enough to accommodate small jets and turboprop planes. Some people arrive on Nevis by air from various destinations, and some people arrive by water, in a yacht or a tall ship perhaps.

Coming over from St. Kitts by water, some visitors arrive at Nevis via the Four Seasons' launch. Others come on an inexpensive ferry from Basseterre, St. Kitts, and some come via a car and passenger ferry (known as the "Sea Bridge") which departs from Majors Bay at the tip of the southeastern peninsula of St. Kitts. Some visitors arrive by water taxi from Turtle Bay on the southeast peninsula.

Tickets for the Basseterre-Charlestown passenger ferries can be purchase at the ferry port in both towns. The cost for two people, as of February, 2013, was $21 (American).

The "Sea Bridge", the Nevis-St Kitts car ferry, also accomodates passengers, in open air seating on the upper level. The "Sea Bridge" ferry dock on St. Kitts is at Majors Bay, which is currently empty of any development at all. The corresponding ferry stop on Nevis is near the main road, but also currently has no businesses right next to it. If you need a taxi, be sure to call and have one waiting for you when you arrive on the island. At the Nevis "Sea Bridge" ferry stop you can easily catch a bus at the main road, less than 100 yards away. The same thing is not true of Majors May, which has no bus service.

Driving

Nevis used to be a British colony, and so people drive on the left hand side of the road, and the one roundabout (traffic circle or rotary) is navigated in a clockwise direction. Drivers from the US may need some time to get used to these differences. The island is so small that it is possible to reach any destination in under half an hour, so why bother rushing?

The overall standard of driving in Nevis is probably no better or worse than it is in London, but unlike London, visitors may encounter a herd of goats or sheep in the middle of the road when they least expect it!

Sometimes visitors may also encounter one of the island's Mack trucks during your stay. These trucks are intimidating enough on a three-lane highway in the US; on the narrow roads of Nevis they appear especially large and noisy.

Ferries

Ferry service is a great way to get from the sister island of St. Kitts over to Nevis. This is particularly true because a number of international flights terminate in St. Kitts. Also some people like to use the ferries for a day trip over to St. Kitts from Nevis. The two islands are quite close together: at their closest point they are only 2 miles apart, across a channel known as "the Narrows". And yet the two islands have quite different atmospheres.

There is a choice of two different ferry services; both of the ferry services are reliable, pleasant, safe, and not expensive. The trip from one island to the other is in both cases a picturesque and scenic ride.

The original ferry services (using the ferry boats Carib Surf, Carib Breeze, Carib Queen, Geronimo, Mark Twain and Sea Hustler) run between the capital cities of these two Caribbean islands, from the harbor in Basseterre in St. Kitts (not far from the St. Kitts airport), all the way over to the dock at Charlestown in Nevis. Most of these ferries take about 30 or 45 minutes and, except for Sea Hustler, they are passenger ferries which do not take cars. They run primarily during the busiest times of the morning and afternoon, when the service is hourly. However from 10 am to 3 pm, during the middle of the day, the service is every two hours. The cost is only US$12 each way, the views are superb, but note that the ferry schedule is variable and a bit unpredictable, so ask at the port, or phone them about times. It is sensible at the very least to consult the supposed schedule for that particular day. Note that this on-line schedule also includes the "Sea Bridge" ferries, which service a different route.

The "Sea Bridge" ferry is a car ferry which also takes pedestrians. It runs a much shorter route across " The Narrows" from Majors Bay near the tip of the southeastern peninsula of St. Kitts, to Cades Bay on the northwestern end of the island of Nevis, and also from Cades Bay over to Majors Bay. This ferry uses two boats, and it can be used to get from the St. Kitts "Bradshaw" airport to Nevis, if you hire a taxi to take you on the picturesque and hilly 20-minute drive from the airport to the ferry slip in Majors Bay. Majors Bay on St. Kitts currently has no businesses, no homes, or any other kind of development, and no bus service. The ferry slip at Cades Bay on Nevis currently has no businesses right at the landing point, so if you are not in a car, you may either want to call and arrange for a taxi in advance, or consider walking 100 yards up to the main road and taking a bus into town, if that is where you want to be.

The "Sea Bridge" ferry trip takes only about 20 minutes. It costs Eastern Caribbean dollars 75 (US$28) for a car and driver one way, EC$125 (US$46) for a car and driver round trip, and EC$25 (US$10) for any other passengers, whether they are on foot or in a car. The "Sea Bridge" runs all day from 8 am to 7 pm, every two hours, except on Wednesdays, when it runs afternoons only.

There is no regular ferry service to other islands in the general area, such as Statia (aka Sint Eustatius), Antigua, or Montserrat, but several times a year the largest ferry boat, the "Sea Hustler" offers a special day trip to one of those islands, usually on a public holiday, and so it is worth asking at the ticket booths to see if anything like that might be available while you are on Nevis. These day trips are certainly not a luxury cruise, far from it, but each one is a curious and interesting adventure.

Getting Around

Nevis has a main road which rings this small Caribbean island; the road is 21 miles in total length. As you travel this ring road, you will notice numerous little side roads, but many of these just go uphill to a few houses and then end.

It's helpful that there are now some official signposts on the island, and Nevis is also starting to get street names, but it can still sometimes be an adventure finding out-of-the-way places. However, there are very good small maps of the island available free at most of the hotels, or from the Tourist Authority, and a really superb, large and detailed O.S. map (last updated in the 1980s) is usually for sale at the museums.

For tourists, taxis are probably the easiest way to get around Nevis: they are vans, so they can easily hold a small group of people, or a whole family. The taxis are quite luxurious, but they can be expensive if you use them a lot.

There are numerous privately-owned but government-licensed buses (these too are vans) which run regular routes on the island, and these are an excellent way to get around, especially at the most popular times of the day. Buses are inexpensive and quite fast, and there may even be a nice shaded bus stop for you to wait in. However, when you want to catch a bus, you can wait anywhere at all on the main road, and just flag the bus down when you see it coming. The bus driver will also drop you off anywhere you want on the main road, and sometimes even up a side road, although if that is off the regular route, this will cost a little extra.

Car rental is another possibility, and renting a bicycle is yet another transportation choice. Before renting a car, it is generally recommended that you first take a taxi tour (or a bus ride) to see where things are, and how people drive on the island (British style, on the left.)

The capital of Nevis, Charlestown, is small enough that it can very easily and pleasantly be explored on foot. The main road around the island is short enough that it too can be biked or hiked instead of driven.

And if you wish to explore some of the many interesting old roadways from previous centuries which are hidden on the mountainside, then hiking is the way to go.

Public Transportation

The public transportation on Nevis consists of community buses; they are all privately owned and operated, but they are licensed by the government.

The buses are convenient, very inexpensive, and easy to use. How do you recognize them? They are nicely-maintained, shiny, new-looking vans, each one of which is decorated with a fanciful name on the front. The never-fail way to tell is that all the buses have a GREEN license plate which starts with the letter "H" or "HA" .

These buses are operated by individuals in the community, and they run according to demand, therefore they don't have a fixed schedule that you could look up somewhere. However, at the times of day when the local people need to get into town or back home again, you will see that the buses run very frequently. The bus driver will gladly stop anywhere at all on the main road to pick up a passenger or drop one off. Let the driver know where you need to go when you get on the bus. If your hotel is off of the main road, you can even ask the bus driver if he will drive you up there as a detour: if the driver is willing it will cost an extremely small extra charge.

The buses are fun and they are a great way to experience West Indian culture, including sometimes some loud music! However, there is no bus schedule, and even though the buses are frequent during the morning when people like to go to market, and in the afternoon when people want to come home from market, buses can be a bit few and far between in the middle of the day or in the evening, and don't run at all after 9 pm.

To get a bus to stop for you, (or to hitch a ride from people, which is quite acceptable on Nevis), stand anywhere at the side of the main road, and when you see a vehicle coming, just wave your hand in a downwards motion. Many ordinary people are very kind and will stop and pick you up if they have room for you. If you flag down a bus but it beeps and drives past you, it simply means that the bus is too full to take on any more passengers.

Taxis or rental cars are the more luxurious way to get around, and rates are in line with other Caribbean destinations. To order a taxi or to find out how to get a rental car, just ask your hotel front desk or whoever is in charge where you are staying.

Of course a pleasant way to travel is simply to go on foot; Nevis really isn't that large, so walking is often a good option. You may be able to walk along the beach to where you want to go, or perhaps instead you can walk beside the road, or roads. Renting a bicycle is another possibility.

It can sometimes be very interesting to walk along trails which were roads in previous centuries, such as the "Upper Round Road" on Nevis. The Upper Round Road trail goes all the way from Golden Rock in the southeast of the island, to Nisbet Plantation in the northeast. You may need a guide to help you find your way on this trail, as not all parts of it are quite clear.

Taxis & Rental Cars

On Nevis, you can always get a taxi: this small Caribbean island has over 100 of them! If you are looking for one, they are not hard to spot: they are well-maintained vans, whose license plates are yellow and begin with the letters "T" or "TA". Some even have a taxi sign on the top of them. Taxis can usually be found waiting near the airport, near the ferry dock, and there is an official taxi stand in Walwyn Square in Charlestown, the capital. You will also sometimes see a taxi driving on the road without a passenger, and then you can wave it down.

The front desk of your hotel will be happy to call a taxi for you whenever you need one (let them know about 20 minutes before you are ready to go), or you can book a taxi for the next day at whatever time is most convenient to you. If you are using the taxi for an outing, you can certainly ask the driver to come back and take you "home" at a fixed time also. (By the way, if you order a taxi from a driver that you especially like, if that person is not available, they all have cellphones and they will call a friend to help out instead.)

When you happen to be out somewhere on the island on foot, taxi drivers will not call out to you, as they do many places in the West Indies, but still, they usually will identify themselves to potential customers.

Should you take a taxi or not? That's your choice. They are a little expensive, but they are quite luxurious.

Rental cars ("R" license plates) are also readily available from several places. You will need the local driver's license, which costs about $20.00 in American money, and the vehicle rental rate will depend upon its size and age, and on the time of year you are renting it. Polaris Rangers are handy if you are going to be off road much for hiking, or for adventure tours to some of the more remote beaches and historic ruins. There are rental companies on the Island that will take you on a guided tour in an open air ranger if you wish. Parking is limited in Charlestown, the capital of Nevis, but parking is easy everywhere else, and free. If you want an easy way to get around, go to the store or a restaurant, you can easily rent a vespa scooter, which makes parking downtown much easier.

Nevis used to be a British island, so you have to drive on the left. (The most dangerous drivers here are visitors from other countries who forget this important fact!) If you are driving and see someone coming directly at you, stop! If you are on the wrong side, they will tell you, and if they are on the wrong side, hopefully they will get back onto the right side!

Should you rent a car? Again, this is your decision. It is perhaps a good idea to take an island tour or some kind of trip in a ranger, so that you can see what the roads are like (and whether you are going to be comfortable with "British driving") before renting a car or scooter. Do remember that although Nevis is small, interesting places to visit are scattered all over the island,

Things to Do in Nevis

Nevis used to be a British colony, and so people drive on the left hand side of the road, and the one roundabout (traffic circle or rotary) is navigated in a clockwise direction. Drivers from the US may need some time to get used to these differences. The island is so small that it is possible to reach any destination in under half an hour, so why bother rushing?

The overall standard of driving in Nevis is probably no better or worse than it is in London, but unlike London, visitors may encounter a herd of goats or sheep in the middle of the road when they least expect it!

Sometimes visitors may also encounter one of the island's Mack trucks during your stay. These trucks are intimidating enough on a three-lane highway in the US; on the narrow roads of Nevis they appear especially large and noisy.

Things to Do

Cades Bay Beach

At the northernmost end of Pinneys Beach is a pleasant bay known as Cades Bay. It is possible to walk from Cades Bay all the way to the outskirts of Charlestown on the beach, only having to leave the sand twice to skirt around rocks. This is three miles of straight beach, which is rather rare in the Caribbean.

Cades Bay is somewhat sheltered, with a low cliff stretching from the middle of the bay to the north end, where the coast comes to a rocky point, which divides this bay from Tamarind Bay, a much smaller bay to the north, which lies between Cades Bay and Cades Point.

The rocky point has been extended out quite some distance into a ramp, and this is where the Sea Bridge ferry docks when it is waiting to take passengers and cars over to Major's Bay in St.

Kitts. There are two ferry boats that come and go between the two destinations every 2 hours. (The ferry ride is fun and scenic, and it is cheap for pedestrians; Major's Bay is worth a short visit on foot, but it is a wild destination and there are no facilities at all there, no bus and no taxis. Of course if you bring your car with you on the ferry you can go wherever you want to on St. Kitts.)

At Cades Bay there is plenty of nice pale-yellowish-grey sand on the beach, and the bottom of the bay is sandy, with only a very few small rocks, thus it is good for swimming. There are several "hot spots" in the bay where thermal volcanic springs bubble up, and these are fun to find!

A hotel which was called "The Inn at Cades Bay" was previously situated right along this narrow strip of land between the road and the bay.

However, since the end of July 2008, the Inn is officially closed. The plan is to convert the site into condominiums, in a development known as "Zenith".

Across the road from Cades Bay is Mansa's farm stand, Mansa's farm itself, and Mansa's terrace restaurant with ocean views. The farm stand carries a very good range of fresh fruits, vegetables, and salad fixings, almost all of which are grown right there on the farm. Mansa is also well-known for his really first-rate fresh-squeezed juices, as well as truly exceptional ginger beer that is homemade from local ginger, and sarsaparilla made with a herb that grows up on the mountain. Mansa's freshly barbequed chicken and ribs are also popular, and ice cream is available for dessert.

Eden Brown Estate

Eden Brown estate is on the west side of the island of Nevis. It is an old ruined sugar plantation, up the hill above the main road.

Eden Brown does not look very different from many other plantation ruins on the island, but this group of ruins has a reputation for being a haunted by the ghost of a young woman who, in the 19th century, was caught up in a tragic incident involving her fiancé and her brother.

Events & Festivals

Nevis, like most small Caribbean islands, has a wealth of events and festivals scattered throughout the year. The two main holidays on Nevis are Christmas and Easter. On Nevis people celebrate Christmas the day before, in Charlestown, until midnight, when everyone goes home to spend Christmas day with their families, and then everyone parties again on Boxing Day (the day after Christmas Day). Easter celebrations stretch from Good Friday, with kite contests, until Easter Monday, with beach parties).

There are other activities spread around the calender, such as the Cycle Club Triathalon (February), Nevis International Cuisine Heritage Exposition (October), and Culturama (July-August). There are also Fishing Tournaments, Horse Racing, Independence Day, and such. All of these usually have music contests and parades associated with them somehow. The best way to check the dates for these events and others, is via the Nevis Tourism Authority site.

The Nevis Olympic/Sprint Triathlon is growing in its appeal to a wider section of the world athletic community. The picturesque Island of Nevis makes a ideal setting for this event, and the event in return enhances Nevis' reputation as a sports tourism destination.

The Nevis Triathlon was voted as one of the top 5 !Must Do! triathlons of 2008, by the prestigious Triathlete magazine website, 2008 also was the 1st time this event was sanctioned by the ITU as a points championship for the recent Olympics.

The Nevis Cycle & Triathlon club, the hosts of the event, take pride in welcoming all their annual visitors. They make sure that the event is both fun and competitive, so whether you are trying to win, want to accomplish a personal goal, or simply want to participate, you are made to feel special and important.

The Triathlon is participated in, and supported by, numerous small businesses and hotels from around the Island; it is truly an island-wide event.

The Nevis Triathlon is permitting members of the Organisation of East Caribbean States (OECS) to vie for the title of OECS Triathlon Champion, Male & Female. These crowns are currently held by Nevisian: Reggie Douglas and Grenadan Clare Morrall.

Horatio Nelson Museum

The Horatio Nelson Museum is a surprisingly rich museum of Nelson memorabilia; in fact this collection is considered to be the best in the New World. In 2005 the museum celebrated the 200th aniversary of the Battle of Trafalgar in which Lord Nelson led 27 British ships to a resounding victory over the Franco-Spanish fleet.

Nevis has a very strong connection historically with Admiral Lord Horatio Nelson, who lived from 1758 to 1805, and who had a brilliant career in the Royal Navy. His inspiring leadership, "The Nelson Touch", and his strategic insights are considered to have been responsible for establishing British supremacy on the high seas.

When he was still a young captain, Nelson was stationed for some time on the island of Nevis, where he met and married a young widow, Fanny Nisbet, whose first husband's family owned Nisbet Plantation. It is very fitting that Nevis should have such a splendid collection, and so many well-pulled together exhibits on this British Naval hero.

Museums & Attractions

Nevis has three museums and numerous other interesting attractions scattered all around the island.

The three small museums are located reasonably close to each other. In the northern end of the Capital, Charlestown, there is the Alexander Hamilton Museum within the stone house which was the birthplace and childhood home of Alexander Hamilton. This museum is located in the ground floor below the assembly room of the Nevis Parliament, which is on the upper floor.

In the middle of Town, the Nevis Government has set up a Sports Museum which is mainly about cricket (the sport of the West Indies).

South of town is the Nelson Museum, named after Horatio Nelson, who as a young sea captain was stationed on Nevis for a while. Here he met and married a young Nevis plantation widow, Fanny Nisbet. Their marriage took place near Montpelier. It takes 25 minutes to walk from the Nelson Museum to the Hamilton Museum at a slow pace, enjoy the 18th and 19th century architecture as you walk along.

One unusual free attraction is the natural volcanic hot spring by the historic Bath Hotel, only a very short walk from town, and just down a dirt path, not at all far off the main road. Just keep asking people along the way to point you in the right direction. It is not far from the Nelson Museum. Here, at an outdoor sheltered bathing spot, you can soak your feet, or if you wish, your whole body, in the very hot, volcanic waters of the Bath Spring.

There is also a small, historic Jewish Cemetery in the centre of town. It is the oldest Jewish Burial Ground in the Caribbean.

All the plantation inns and hotels have their own lovely gardens, and approximately 3 miles above town is the Botanical Garden of Nevis, which is near Montpelier. This botanical garden is of moderate size, and it is very nicely put together, with beautiful views.

There are over 53 churches on Nevis (many historic, some dating back to 1643), each with their own architecture, paintings, or style, and they are to be found in the local communities. All of the churches welcome visitors and are nice to see.

Nevis Island Government set up Heritage Village which is small, quaint and unique to the

Caribbean. The Village shows you all the different building styles that have been used in Nevis' past, and they also make and sell local wine. The Heritage Village is not Williamsburg or Jametown, VA, but it is nonetheless interesting.

Many ruins of old sugar estates are found along the roadside and hidden up the mountain, and at Coconut Walk, an old lime kiln is crumbling into the sea.

Nightlife

Nevis is one Caribbean destination where night life is mainly on the quiet side; unlike many places in the West Indies, Nevis has no casinos, few discos, and is not known for loud parties.

However, there are special events such as Culturama, in late July and early August, which includes music and dancing until the wee hours, and there are also lively celebrations at Christmas and Easter. But people do not really come to Nevis for the nightlife. That said, there are a few places to go and things to do on a regular basis:

Four Seasons almost always has a band playing down by the Cabana and, as long as they aren't running full, anyone can go. If you get there and they are full, walk down the beach to either Sunshine's Bar for Killer Bees, or keep walking to Chevy's for a Stinger. They have Dinner & Karaoke Fun every Monday from 6.30pm, and "Reggae Nights" every Sunday with a local DJ.

In Charlestown, locals may be hanging out by Night Moves where you will be welcome. V's Courtyard is open on Friday and Saturday nights featuring Live Bands and DJ's. Eddy's, upstairs on the main square of Charlestown, has a Happy

Hour on Wednesday nights which becomes a celebration lasting many hours.

There are also Thursday night beach BBQs with live music at Nisbet Plantation, pig roasts at The Hermitage, and a steel drum band some evenings at Oualie Beach Hotel. Golden Rock has a string band some evenings on Saturdays. If you wish to attend any of these events at the hotels, please do call and confirm first, as they are not always available, and even when they are available, space is limited.

Maybe instead you prefer a quiet and beautiful "nightlife"? Why not? This can include strolling on the beach, stargazing by a campfire, or even going to look for Sea Turtles, which frequently nest on Nevis beaches

Shopping

Unlike some larger Caribbean islands, Nevis is not famous for its shopping, unless perhaps you or someone you know is interested in stamps? if so, there is a Philatelic Bureau on Market Street in the center of Charlestown where you can browse a very wide selection of unusual and interesting Nevis stamps, or if you prefer, you can contact the Bureau at philbur@caribusurf.com.

Other than that, you may have to explore a little in order to find good shopping on Nevis, however, for a very easy start, your hotel may quite likely have a small shop or souvenir room which may only be open when a guest requests it.

If you go into Charlestown, the main town, you will find that there are a few shops that have clothing, dolls and other interesting souvenir items, however it's important to bear in mind that the stores are only open from 8 am until 4 pm on weekdays, that Saturdays are half-days, and that all the shops are closed on Sundays. This is because the owners want to spend lots of time with their families. All in all, Nevis is not really a shopping mecca in any sense of the word, but this being understood, there are some nice things to buy.

The Newcastle Pottery at the northeast end of the island is interesting and worth a visit. The Pottery has been there for centuries. They still make nice pottery items out of Nevis clay, and fire them the traditional way, using coconut husks and grass.

As for artwork, you can buy the work of local Nevis artists at The Riviere House.

And a sculptor named Robert Humphreys, works in bronze or silver, and displays his sculpture pieces at Zetlands, in Gingerland, the southern end of Nevis.

In any case, this all adds up to the fact that there is no one single centralized location for shopping, but there are a lot of nice things to find here and there, so shopping on Nevis can be cool, because it becomes another adventure!

Sports & Activities

Like many small Caribbean islands, Nevis does not really have American football or baseball, but there are nonetheless a lot of different sport activities available which enthusiasts can enjoy.

Most of the hotels have tennis courts; the Four Seasons has clay courts as well as paved ones. As for golf, there is of course the world-class Robert

Trent Jones Golf Course (at the Four Seasons resort), but there is another small course dating from the 1960's at Jones Estate, and in addition a private homeowner put in a Pitch and Putt on his property to encourage visitors. Neither of these last two are very serious, but both are fun.

As for spectator sports, visitors are certainly always welcome to go to the community cricket pitches to watch the games. Cricket is a much-loved sport in the West Indies, and if you go along to watch, the players may quite likely try to convince you to join in with them! The same applies to soccer and basketball.

Nevis is unusual in that it is one of the few places in the Caribbean which has a Racetrack with regularly scheduled horse races; these are very lively events which attract a lot of people. They are lots of fun to attend, and they feature high-quality horses.

There are also several other available activities, such as hiking: which ranges from the very easy rain forest hikes, through exploring hidden ruins and bat caves, all the way up to the very strenuous Nevis Peak climb. Three places on Nevis offer horseback riding, all with different views and trails. Land-based people may also want to try mountain biking: the Mountain Biking Club even holds a Triathalon.

Water Sports people will find that even thought the beaches are not white powdered sand, still the coastline of Nevis provides good snorkelling, kayaking, windsurfing, scuba diving, and very good fishing. Strong experienced swimmers may want to try one of the Cross-Narrows Swims, which are held twice yearly, but if you do decide to try this challenging swim on your own, please hire a kayak to follow along in case you tire out.

As for nature activities, Nevis is very rich in nature. Over 130 kinds of birds can be found in various enviroments around the island, as well as over 60 species of butterflies, many of which can be seen on the hiking trips. Lovely tropical flowers adorn the landscape, not only at the hotels, botanical gardens and in resident's gardens, even in the villages, but there are a lot of very interesting wild flowers too, including 23 minute species of orchids, which are hidden up the mountainside in with the Heliconias.

Wild Monkeys

Nevis is one of very few Caribbean islands which have a large population of wild monkeys. They are African Green Vervet Monkeys, and they also live on St. Kitts and on Barbados. These monkeys were first brought to the islands as pets in the 17th or 18th centuries. Some escaped or were set free, and they managed to establish themselves very well in the wild.

They are large, handsome monkeys with extremely long tails, and they spend a lot of time on the ground. Their greenish-beige coats are good camouflage, and this makes them hard to spot. The face and ears are black, but the fringe of hair around their face is a creamy white, as is their whole underside. The males are bigger than the females: a large male monkey can weigh 45 pounds, and be over 3 feet tall when standing upright to look around, as they sometimes do.

There are literally thousands of monkeys on Nevis; they live in troops or tribes, each troop consisting of about 20 to 70 individuals of all different ages, with an adult monkey serving as the leader. The troops spend their nights sleeping in trees, in the more inaccessible parts of the forest on the steeper slopes of the mountain. Twice a day, usually in the early morning and the late afternoon, each troop will range out from its home base looking for food, which is mostly small seeds and fruits. (They especially enjoy unripe green mangoes which they eat like apples.) Each troop travels on its own territory, varying the route a little each day to ensure better foraging.

Some monkey troops go all the way down to the beaches, often traveling in the Ghauts or ravines both for secrecy and for the availablity of fresh water.

At the right times of day you may glimpse monkeys almost anywhere on Nevis, for example, on the Four Seasons Golf Course. And although the monkeys generally prefer to stay away from people, they are extremely interested in gardens, farms, and fruit trees of every kind. In fact the monkeys are a major problem for anyone on the island (farmer or householder) who is trying to grow fruit or vegetables.

Probably the most reliable area on Nevis for visitors to see monkeys is in the grounds of Golden Rock Hotel, especially in or near the mango and citrus trees, either early in the morning or in the later afternoon around tea time. If you are lucky enough to come across the troop in a quiet place where you can sit and watch them for an hour or so, you will be amazed to see their highly organized social structure, and if you are close enough, you will hear a wide range of quiet vocalizations as they communicate with one another.

Family Travel

Nevis, West Indies, is very family-oriented and is a very safe destination for small children in every way. All restaurants will have something suitable for the whole family. That said, there are some things parents should be aware of.

Do's include:

Make sure your hotel allows small children and has places for them to run. Golden Rock has a nature trail, but the swimming pool is very deep, even in the shallow end. Four Seasons tries to put families and singles on seperate ends when possible, and the resort even has separate pools.

Nature excursions are very child-friendly, and several are suitable for all ages. This includes hiking with trained ecologists, snorkeling with marine biologists, or wandering around looking for monkeys. These are educational opportunities not found in many other Caribbean islands.

Take an island tour in a taxi, and let everyone see the whole of Nevis. Stop somewhere during the tour different from where you are staying and get a nice cold drink, or perhaps lunch or afternoon tea.

The Family Nature Trail at Golden Rock is good for short tours and you will often be able to see monkeys in the mornings and in the afternoons: it's free!

Don'ts are:

Don't let your kids go up to baby donkeys: they may be very cute, but the donkey mother will defend her young.

Don't leave your young children unattended near the sea, for obvious reasons.

Don't pick unknown plants, this is not wise, as some children (and even adults) can have allergic reactions to a few kinds of tropical plants.

Generally Nevis is a very safe place, even the bars are safe on Nevis, so go ahead and bring the children!

Off the Beaten Path

In the Caribbean, a lot of visitors like to relax on the beach and do very little at all, and many visitors never even eat a meal outside of their hotel. On Nevis less than 2% of visitors climb

Nevis Peak (grant you it is quite a challenging hike), and only 10-15% of visitors venture on the easier outings up the lower slopes of the mountain. And yet in Nevis there are a myriad of interesting little places off of the beaten path, and they are all just waiting for people who like a change of scenery and a small adventure.

For local food, check out Rumours, Pemo's, Mingles, or even the Yellow Bus by the dock (they have great saltfish cakes). V's Courtyard in town is hopping on Saturday nights. Most of these places are frequented mainly by locals, medical students, and only a few other visitors.

For those who are wanting some "Indiana Jones" kind of adventures, check out the ruins at Mount Pleasant: few locals even know how to find these! There are also hidden ruins at Montravers, Eden Browne Estate, and even close to Chevy's Calypso Bar. Can you hike up and find the old cistern filled with Talapia up at Tower Hill? There are great views from there as well.

Some adventures you may need guides for, but some can be found on your own. This island in the West Indies still needs discovering!

First-time Visitors

Something that first-time visitors to this little spot in the Caribbean might want to bear in mind is, that because you are on vacation, hopefully the word "fast" is not essential to your vocabulary...

Most things on Nevis move at a slow pace, and you may possibly encounter a few waiting lines, because everyone here still takes their time, and chats. If you like things to move fast, and are looking for fast night life, fast casinos, or even fast women, you should probably go somewhere else; the only thing that's fast on Nevis is the Horse Racing, and even at the Racetrack there's a lot of time between races to relax.

During your first trip, definitely take an island tour. This takes you all the way around the island, and you can see how big 36 square miles really is. It will also help you plan what else you want to see. Shoppers might want to check out the numerous small places hidden around Charlestown. History buffs will probably want to go to the Museums, the various Plantation Inns, the other historical sites, and perhaps also to the Nevis Heritage Village.

On your tour you will also start to see that much of Nevis is "bush". On that mountain there is a lovely rain forest for hiking into, and there is lots of interesting 19th century sugar-extracting machinery hidden in the shrubbery. Adventure and lovely views await as you visit all the different beaches. Snorkeling and diving on Nevis may not be the absolute best in the West Indies, but it's up there with them.

Restaurants? Your choice. A popular local casual spot would be Sunshine's, and another great beach bar is Chevy's Beach Bar, both located on Pinney's Beach.

For a special occasion, any of the hotels will be glad to accomodate whatever you need (as long as it is legal).

The Performing Arts

This Caribbean destination has very little in the way of high-culture "Performing Arts": there is no opera, no theaters as yet, and not too much in the way of concerts. Nevis is primarily a community-based culture, where people go to churches to hear gospel singing, and go to schools to see plays which star their children and friends.

There is however a Nevis Theater Guild with its own writers and directors.

Although this is a small island, some performers here are extremely good, for example, there really are talented singers at some of the churches, and visitors are always welcome! It's great for people who love 'that old time gospel music'.

There are occasional music concerts, usually associated with holidays such as Christmas and Culturama. A lot of singers make up their own songs, which are usually based on something happening in the community. Thus, songs which satirize local politicians are quite popular, and the songwriters will also happily make fun of world leaders as well! The style of these local songs is primarily either Reggae or Calypso. These concerts start late, and often run until the wee hours of the morning.

Adventure Activities

Nevis is excellent for people who love nature and want to explore; there are a lot of different things to do on the island if you are adventurous and love the outdoors.

Several possibilities involve exploring the rain forest, or hiking up into old ruins hidden on the mountainside. Most of these hikes take two or three hours, and some outings are more rugged than others. If you would like to go on one of the more challenging hikes, please expect to get a little dirt or mud on your clothes. If you are a really fit and adventurous hiker, you may want to try climbing all the way to the top of Nevis Peak and back, which takes 4 to 6 hours.

For less rugged adventurers, there are free trails around the Golden Rock Hotel area; you can get a map for these from the hotel office. (Actually all the trails on Nevis are free, it's just that for some outings you have to have the help of a guide to find your way there and back.)

But maybe you prefer to be 'sitting down' for your adventures? OK, then you should try mountain biking or horse riding; both of these are available on Nevis. Bikes can either be rented or used as part of a guided tour. When you are horse riding you will need a guide with you.

Want another sitting adventure sport? How about trying kayaking? Birdwatchers may even want to kayak out to a small offshore island where many seabirds nest, but you need to be fit to do this, because it is quite hard work to get there and back!

But even sitting down, do these activities sounds like too much work? Then find out when they have the next horse races on Nevis; going to the races is also an adventure: the thundering of the hooves and the enthusiastic placing of bets should generate some excitement for you.

And finally, if even that is too much excitement, just sit around the hotels or bars and watch the butterflies or birds there, there's still plenty of interesting things to see...

Biking and Hiking

This small but very picturesque Caribbean island is really ideal for both hiking and biking. Biking is a particularly convenient way to get around: it's the best way to see some of the smaller villages, and there are good bike trails that cross the landscape of Nevis. Hiking paths are found in even more places all over the island, on flatter, hilly, or even mountainous terrain. At Golden Rock Hotel you can pick up hand-outs for some self-guided hiking trails which start there, up at 1,000 feet, where it is never too hot.

Cycling is easy on Nevis. Much of the main road is flat, unless you are staying up on the mountain, and most of the road has recently been improved and resurfaced. The road does not have a separate bike lane, but it's not as narrow as on many islands, and does not carry a lot of traffic. There is a bike rental company on the island that has a wide range of equipment and offers a lot of different guided tours. You can simply rent the equipment and get advice there, but they also have what you might need for repairs. The bike rental company can help you learn about the old Estate roads, and they can tell you about hazards for mountain bikers (watch out for mother goats). There are other places to get bikes, but none of the others at present have anywhere near the selection or quality.

Eden Brown Estate

The Eden Brown ruins, which are on the Mannings Estate, on the island of Nevis, are considered to be a haunted ruin, because of a tragedy that happened there in the early 19th century, which left a beautiful young woman without a husband, and possibly without a brother too.

The ruins of Eden Brown's Great House, and other associated buildings, are located on the eastern side of the island of Nevis, not far off of the Main Road, near Butler's Village.

On moonlit nights, local people still report hearing the sobbing and wailing of the ghost of the forlorn bride-to-be, as she walks through the ruins, wearing her wedding dress.

Fish Bowl

This dive site is a large, bowl-shaped area of sand within the coral reef, at 70 foot depth. There are sea fans and sponges nearby, as well as a lot of fish.

Beautiful Flying Gurnards with their strange blue-tinted 'wings' live on the sand in Fish Bowl. It's also a great place to see lobsters, which hide out along the cracks in the coral rock. But most of all, the place is just really full of fish: there are great shoals of Grey and Yellow Snapper, Angel Fish and Grunts, all of which swim among the divers and make you feel as if you are flying with flocks of colorful birds.

To dive this location and any of the other dive sites mentioned, you must go with a Certifed Diving Operator and Nevis only has one.

Fort Ashby

The name Fort Ashby refers to a small fortified area on the Caribbean coast of Nevis, south of Cades Bay but north of the lagoon at Cotton Ground. The fort was the first of many fortifications built by the British in the 1600s, to defend Nevis against attacks from rival nations. These simple fortifications were not really much to speak of: they were often nothing more than a small outpost with just a few men and a few cannons in the right spot. North of Fort Ashby was another defended spot called Pelican Point, which is now a private house.

All that remains of Fort Ashby itself are some cannon and some sections of wall. One interesting fact is that Fort Ashby was originally right on the coast, with the outer wall bordering the sea, but now it is some distance inland. (Much of Nevis is losing land due to coastal erosion, but in this area, the coast has been added to over the centuries by the sea depositing sand here.)

Fort Ashby itself is at best only a very minor attraction, and it is rather hard to locate, but as people drive past this area on the main road they may find it interesting to see the freshwater lagoon which lies between the small village of Cotton Ground and the beach. This lagoon is formed by the water from Nelson's Spring. It served as a very convenient source of fresh water for sailing ships in the past. The lagoon has flowering water lilies, and originally supported a wide variety of birds, butterflies and aquatic life.

Geo Caches

Geo Caching is about locating hidden Geographical "Treasure Chests" using GPS coordinates, (in other words Latitudes and Longitudes.) The Treasure Chests or Geo Caches each contain a Log Book to register in, with other odds and ends included as bonuses.

The team has hidden 5 Geo Caches at historically significant places on the island of Nevis. Any visitor can locate the caches, and then learn about the Pirates that came through this part of the Caribbean.

There is also an ink pad and stamp in each cache. Use these to stamp a special sheet (email geocache2008@live.com and ask for one, it is free). If a visitor collects all five stamps on their sheet, many places on Nevis will give that person either free drinks, or other discounts. This includes discounts on hiking, biking, dinners, car rentals, scuba diving and even taxis. The sheet will also contain more information and links for Nevis.

Group Activities

Looking for places for a group to come visit in the Caribbean? Trying to find an exotic locale for that family reunion or wedding?

What can Nevis offer?

The Four Seasons Resort and Mount Nevis Hotel both offer conference packages for really large groups, but all of the smaller hotels can also accommodate a wedding, a family reunion, or parties of friends. Contact the individual hotel websites for more information on these deals.

What other activities are available for bigger groups of people once they are here?

Many of the various available group activities are, in general, better able to handle reasonably-sized groups of people rather than very large numbers, but most organizers can go out several times in succession when needed. Here are some possibilities: hiking in groups usually goes out with one guide per 10 people, mountain biking is good for up to 15; as for horse riding, groups of 10 can easily be arranged. Taxi tours usually use minivans and some large vans can take up to 15 people. Water sports include sailing for 6 people, snorkelling for 6 to 20 people, fishing for 6 people, and scuba diving for up to 20.

Monkey Shoal

Monkey Shoal is a fine area for fishing or scuba diving. In fact, many different dives are possible here, because Monkey Shoal is two square miles of Caribbean reef, varying in depth from less than 40 feet to 100 feet.

The area usually has excellent visibility of more than 100 feet. This is a place where you can find good full growths of Pillar Coral and Elkhorn Coral, and large Brain Corals. The fish at Monkey Shoal include Glass Eyed and Yellow Tailed Snappers, French and Grey Angelfish, Nurse Sharks and Black Tip Reef Sharks.

Nevis Cycle and Triathlon Club

Formed on a whim more than 10 years ago, the Nevis Cycle & Triathlon Club continues to go from strength to strength, and the club has created a number of events that attract visitors from around the globe.

If you are a triathlete, road biker, mountain biker, swimmer or runner, the club welcomes you to join in any or all of their regular training sessions.

If you are feeling competitive they also host two major triathlons each year, plus a series of minitriathlons, a cross-channel swim, a round the island run, and a number of road and mountain bike races, so, if you need an excuse for a vacation, they can supply it.

For more information about the club, its members, and their schedule of activities

Peppered Pickled Pirates Party Time!

Peppered Pickled Pirate Party Time is a relatively new event for Nevis in the Caribbean. The event combines two things the Caribbean is known for: hot peppers and pirates; it promotes local history and culture, and it's really about having a good time. The event was launched in the autumn of 2009, when it ran at two times, first accommodating the British and European school vacation time from October 25 through October

31, and then after that, American Thanksgiving, November 22 through November 28.

Nevis has a lot of genuine pirate history. Famous pirate Captain Kidd got his start on Nevis by stealing a French ship from St. Kitts, after which the British Governor paid him for it. Perhaps surprisingly, Kidd used the money to help set up churches in New York City. His number two man, Hendrick van der Haul, is reported to have been "a small black man"; pirate crews were often 30% African, and these were true crew members and not slaves. There were many other pirates that visited this small Caribbean island, including "Black Bart", Bartholomew Sharpe, Edward Lowe, and the notorius François L'Ollonais. Horatio Nelson wasn't exactly a pirate, but he came to the island to stop Nevis from trading with the American colonies!

This festival is quite different from the normal music and food celebrations found throughout the West Indies. It started off with a "Pirate Invasion" of sailing vessels racing over from the neighbouring island of St. Kitts carrying Pirates into the harbour at Charlestown, with Pirate Flags flying. That night there was an Admiral's dinner at Montpelier Plantation Inn with dart throwing, handmade darts and a wine cork board.

There was a Pepper Sauce Contest for the local ladies, which was held at the Handicraft House. Nevis is already famous for its excellent pepper sauce, so the best of the best was really worth sampling.

One hotel, The Hermitage Inn, hosted a party where all the food items started with the letter "p": a pig roast with potatoes and pumpkin soup, served with a pirate punch! Sounds delicious! Everyone who came to the party dressed as something that starts with the letter "p", thus dressing as pirates, priests, palm trees, penguins, pink elephants or postage stamps, were all possibilities! The most unusual costume won dinner for free.

Golden Rock Inn, had a Crew Carousal, singing pirate songs, and a contest for the best pirate joke, so watch out, Jack Sparrow! Mount Nevis Hotel did a West Indian night with Conch Horn blowing. Nisbet Plantation hosted "a "roaring rum mixer". This was not a bartenders' contest, but a curiosity: everyone brings something which gets mixed with rum to see what happens! A beach barbecue follows. Hurricane Cove Bungalows also helped sponsor activities.

Peppered Pickled Pirates Party Time is a lot more than just food and singing. A Family Day at Oualie Beach Resort raised money for local charities. There was a poker race on bikes, a pirate pitch for marine education, and raffles of locally made art for the Change Centre for Single Mothers. There was an island-wide treasure hunt, with a treasure chest hidden around the island. Clues were given out on the radio, and posted at the hotels. There was also a water fight, where people brought water balloon bombs and squirt guns.

Since the ocean was calm enough, there was a Scuba dive to the ocean floor to look at the sunken remains of an old ship. There was also horse racing, and a Donkey Derby to raise funds for the Animal Rescue Centre.

This is a fun festival, rather than a fancy one, and it will take place in 2011 and subsequent years, so please contact one of the organisers for more details, or to give suggestions. Organizers can be contacted at organizers@piratesofnevis.com

Rainy Day Activities

Nevis would like to say that the weather will be perfect during your stay, however everyone has a different idea of what 'perfect weather' is! When it is sunny and bright most people do like to be on the beach or in the sea, but what if there is a rainstorm, or even in the Caribbean, a hurricane? (They are not that common -- although the west coast of Nevis was brushed with the surges from Omar last year, Nevis has not had to deal with a hurricane full on since 1999.)

For rainy days, most of the hotels have a television in their lounge (many hotels do not have televisions in the rooms) and they will also have a library of books, as well as games (checkers, chess, dominoes, etc). There are probably also some videos/DVDs. The book titles are constantly being changed, not by the hotels but by other guests. Whatever you are interested in, you can usually find a fellow enthusiast to talk to, and spend a pleasant day making new friends. Four Seasons offers rainy day programmes in their lobby and these are usually open to all.

Rainy days are also the perfect time for that spa treatment you were thinking about. There's nothing like a massage or facial to make the day seem brighter. There are several spas on the island -- Four Seasons, The Palms at Nisbet

Plantation and Compassionate Touch -- just to name a few. Visiting one or two of the Nevis museums could also make a rainy day more interesting.

Still want to get out? Try hiking up into the Rain Forest; it is after all a "rain" forest, there are some easy trails, and getting wet is really no big deal in a tropical climate. You may also want to walk the beaches: rough waves wash things ashore, so it's a great time to look for shells and to collect beach glass. Maybe you could take a trip out and visit some of the local "rum shops"? Rum shops in the Caribbean are not liquor stores; they are pleasant, small, local community bars, which often serve food too.

Rainy days on Nevis are usually not rainy all day, and even during major storms the weather will clear up for short periods. But enjoy the rain, it's always warm rain, and after all, this is what keeps the island so green and clean.

Sea Turtles

Sea turtles are fairly commonly seen in the waters around Nevis, and right now the coastline of the island is just undeveloped enough that it is still a valuable nesting site for three endangered species of marine turtles: Green Sea Turtles, Hawksbills, and Leatherbacks. These extraordinary and fascinating animals are as old as the dinosaurs, but to survive into the future, both the turtles themselves and their nesting habitats require protection. This is especially true of the Leatherbacks, which are the largest turtles in the world, and the most endangered too.

On Nevis the main nesting season for the sea turtles is from February through October, but a few have been seen nesting as late as December. The turtles require a sand beach with not too steep a slope, and it needs to be a quiet stretch where they will not be disturbed while they are egg-laying.

On the website mentioned below you can see the travels of two different Hawksbill Turtles over the time period from August 2006 to February 2007. During those 6 months, one turtle named "Nevis" swam almost 400 miles between the islands of Nevis and St. Martin, and another turtle, "Mango", swam more than 1,500 miles almost all the way to the Yucatan Peninsula of Mexico! These turtles were tracked by the Caribbean Conservation Corporation and the Sea

Turtle Survival League. www.cccturtle.org/satellitetra...

St. Thomas' Lowland Church

The Parish church of St. Thomas' Lowland stands on a hill overlooking the Caribbean Sea and St. Kitts. The church was built in 1643, and was the first Anglican church in the Caribbean.

The churchyard has gravestones which go as far back as 1649, with the graves of the first British settlers of Nevis, and the church itself contains the vault of the founder of the Bath Hotel, John Huggins, who lived from 1763 to 1821.

This church originally served Jamestown, which was the first capital of Nevis. Jamestown no longer exists as a settlement, and archeologists are currently working to try to determine why it was abandoned. An old legend tells of

Jamestown having sunk under the sea after an earthquake and a tidal wave. The archeologists now think that the earthquake and resulting tidal wave may have covered Jamestown in sand.

The Thermal Vents

Caribbean scuba divers may enjoy this area, which shows off one of Nevis' specialities: at 90 feet there is a volcanic 'hot vent' or underwater 'fumarole', where emerging volcanic gases heat the water to boiling-point, and a column of hot water full of small bubbles rises to the surface. This is something that many divers will not have seen before.

The extra heat encourages growth, and accounts for the adundant marine life found here, including some very large lobsters. The underwater landscape at this dive spot includes a reef which drops steeply off from 35 to 95 feet. Lots of Spotted Drum hang out in the overhangs, along with High Hats and Arrow Crabs. Large Black Coral trees grow out of the side of the reef.

The Wreck of the 'River Taw'

Scuba divers will probably be keen to visit the wreck of this large freighter, which was rated by Skin Diver Magazine as being in the top 20 in the Caribbean. The 144 foot ship sank in a storm in 1985, and then, four years later, the sunken ship was broken in half during Hurricane Hugo.

The two parts of the wreck lie in 50 feet of water. The surfaces are beautifully encrusted with coral, and both parts of the wreck are home to numerous fish, including Angelfish, Rays, Snappers and Squirrel Fish.

DIvers who wish to visit Nevis should be aware that there is only one dive operator on the whole island, and the staff there schedule requests on a first-come, first-served, basis. To get a chance to dive this site, email the dive center at: info@scubanevis.co

Wanna Get Married?

Do you want a wedding without all of the hullabaloo? Would you maybe like to dress formally for the biggest event of your life and yet still go barefoot?

Many of the hotels on Nevis offer wedding packages which include a wedding coordinator, photographer, cake, champagne, flowers, and even witnesses if needed..

But you don't have to have the ceremony performed at a hotel. The marriage ceremony can take place almost anywhere on this Caribbean island (on the beach, in the hills, in a church, etc) and Officers of the Court known as Magistrates can perform the ceremony, unless you would prefer a member of the clergy.

Wedding coordinators who live and work on the island can make your planning and preliminaries hassle-free, by accompanying you to Charlestown to complete the necessary paperwork and such. They can also help you select your choice of site for the exchange of your vows.

There are a few requirements: one is that you must be on-island at least two business days prior to the wedding date. another one is that you must have with you the necessary documents. You will need your passport and birth certificate. If you have been married before, you will also need to bring the correct legal documents to demonstrate your status as an unmarried person, and people who have never been married before will need a notarized statement confirming that they are single.

Whether it's just the bride and groom, or an entire entourage of family and friends, Nevis is a good place for that perfect wedding and honeymoon and the rest of the marriage is up to you!

Whale Watching

Nevis is not well known for whale watching, but it is a possibility at two main times during the year. The first is during March and April, when migrating whales pass through the general area heading south, and the second is late October through early December when the whales are heading back north.

There are over 30 species of cetaceans that are found in the Caribbean, but most are not easy to see. The whales that can sometimes be seen in this part of the Leeward Islands include Humpback whales, Sperm whales, Pygmy Sperm whales, and Pilot whales, as well as several different kinds of dolphins.

In general however, it is worth saying that you are quite likely to see turtles and dolphins off of Nevis, but not so likely to see whales.

Bike Nevis

Bike Nevis runs guided mountain bike tours in Nevis, and they also provide mountain bike and road bike rentals . Bike tours are available for the beginner, advanced and expert biker.

Nevis itself is a beautiful Caribbean island with large central dormant volcano, and this gives the island a very varied landscape: some of it steep and some less so, some of it wild and some less so. There are a wide variety of bike tracks and trails, both single and double, and even though Nevis is not a large island, there are plenty of routes available such that somone can enjoy several hours, or even several days, of biking, without ever getting bored, or going the same way twice.

Botanical Gardens of Nevis

Nevis is fortunate that is has so many exceptional attractions, and the Botanical Gardens is one of the best of them. The site is about eight acres, reasonably high up in Montpelier Estates, and it has lovely views down to the sea in the distance. The gardens are already mature and very well laid out, with fountains and sculptures of monkeys, birds and so on, and an impressive collection of Asian sculptures scattered throughout.

This cleverly designed place is very charming and interesting to walk through, and is divided into many sections, each one of which has its own character, including an Events Garden with fountains and vines which is often used for weddings, shady orchid terraces with bromelliads and Spanish moss, a succulent garden, a good variety of tropical fruit trees, waterlily pools, and a large Rainforest Conservatory with parrots and a Mayan style "ruin", which has been recently renovated to include a Butterfly Garden. Also newly added is a bee-keeping area to produce local honey.

The Garden also has the large and very well-stocked Galleria Gift shop, a branch of the well-known upscale World Art & Antiques Gallery on the island of Anguilla, soon to open another branch in Nevis at the famous Eva Wilkin Mill in Gingerland. The Gardens Gift Shop is located inside the ground floor of the elegant traditional Caribbean plantation Great House building. A restaurant is located on the top floor of this building with sweeping views of the mountain and panoramic sea views, but if you plan to eat there, do call ahead first to make sure it is open.

Cottle Church

The ruins of Cottle Church are off the main road at Round Hill Estate, in the woods, in the northern part of the island of Nevis, not far from the airport.

This very small church or chapel, also known as "St. Mark's of Ease", was built in 1824 by John Cottle, who was Nevisian Island President at that time.

John Cottle built the church specifically so that his family and slaves could worship together under one roof, which was a controversial idea at the time. Anyone else who also wished to attend was warmly welcomed.

Eva Wilkin Galleria at Gingerland

Eva Wilkin was a very accomplished Caribbean artist, whose work has become quite valuable. Although trained in England, she lived on Nevis for 50 years, and in addition to her paintings, she created several murals of Nevis scenes. She excelled at rather penetrating portraits, especially of local children.

Wilkin's studio is in a picturesque location, an 18th century windmill on the hillside near Clay Ghaut in Gingerland. The artist passed away in 1989, but her studio is now an excellent gallery which, in addition to selling prints of her work, also shows works from other Nevis artists, and has its own art-related gift shop.

Open 10-3pm M-F or by appointment, but call and check, as it may have changed hours.

Fig Tree Church

This small Caribbean church (aka St. John's Figtree Church) is perhaps best known for its church register, in which is recorded the marriage of Horatio Nelson to Frances Nisbet, as follows:

"1787 March 11th. Horatio Nelson, Esquire. Captain of His Majesty's Ship the Boreas, to Frances Herbert Nisbet, Widow."

The church, St. John's Figtree, is located between the villages of Fig Tree and Church Ground, which are on the main road about two miles east of Charlestown, in the southern part of the island of Nevis. The church was originally built in the 1680s; however the current building dates from 1838. The churchyard has many gravestones dating from the 17th century.

Four Seasons Tennis Centre

The tennis complex at the Four Seasons Resort on Nevis is impressive and well-equipped. There are four red-clay courts and six hard courts, including one show court with wooden benches under a wood roof. Two of the hard courts and two of the clay courts, are lit for night play. The tennis pros and general staff at Four Seasons are widely regarded as excellent.

On Nevis most tennis enthusiasts will probably want to play in the early morning or the later afternoon, because the sun during the middle of the day can be quite intense. But fortunately, although Nevis is tropical, it has almost constant cooling ocean breezes from the Caribbean, which means that it is never extremely hot.

Gingerland Methodist Church

You can't help noticing Gingerland Methodist Church as you drive on the main road through St. George Gingerland parish; right beside the road you will see a very large, impressive, rather handsome, cut-stone building of an unusual octagonal form. It was built in 1844.

When the Methodists arrived on Nevis they believed that the slaves should be taught to read, so that they might understand the Bible in particular. The Methodists taught classes in English and religion, despite some strong opposition from the plantation owners.

Montpelier House

Montpelier House, Nevis, was where Horatio Nelson and Frances Nisbet celebrated their marriage, on March 11th 1787. Unfortunately the great plantation house itself no longer stands, and currently only the original stone gate posts mark the site. However, very close to the site is Montpelier Plantation Inn, which is itself well worth looking at.

Montpelier Plantation Inn includes several historic buildings, and is an excellent inn with a restaurant that serves first-rate cuisine.

Nearby on what used to be the old plantation estate is the Botanical Garden of Nevis, another place which is very much worth a visit.

Nelson fans can also visit Fig Tree Church, where the Nelson marriage ceremony was officially recorded; there is a copy of the original certificate on view.

Montravers Great House

Mountravers Estate was a Nevis plantation that produced sugar for export for 300 years; the buildings of the estate are on the mountainside, directly above Pinney's Beach. Mountravers is the one of the best documented plantation estates in the Caribbean. The plantation was owned in 1708 by Azariah Pinney (after whom Pinneys Beach is named) and by successive generations of the Pinney family until it was sold in 1815.

There are extensive ruins of very considerable historical interest at Mountravers, and these ruins are being restored. The estate's Great House is stone, and dates from the early 19th century. It is a grand building, three-stories high, and was occupied right up until the 1950s. Fortunately, in the case of this estate, a great deal of the original papers have survived from the plantation days, and are in archives in Bristol, England. These papers make the site all that much more interesting and valuable, both historically and archeologically.

Nelson's Lookout

Nelson's Lookout is a Caribbean fort up on Saddle Hill, a large, saddle-shaped hill (one of several ancient volcanic cores) in the southern part of the island of Nevis. You will need a guide to lead you up to Nelson's Lookout, because Saddle Hill Fort is overgrown with scrub, although many of the old stone walls are still visible.

This is the point from which Nelson reportedly used to check the ocean for ships coming from the south; he was watching for Spanish and French ships, which might have meant trouble, as well as for other British ships.

Back then, the old main road around the island, the "Lower Round Road", used to follow the coastline of Nevis, even going around south of Saddle Hill, but that strip of land has partly been lost to marine erosion.

Nevis Peak Hike

Nevis Peak is the volcanic mountain which in ancient times created the island of Nevis. The peak rises to over three thousand feet, and it is quite often surrounded by cloud at the very top, even in the middle of the day.

The steepest parts of the mountain are covered in rain forest, and at the highest altitudes, cloud forest. The peak makes a beautiful backdrop to almost all activities on Nevis, and is one of the many things that makes Nevis so picturesque. The peak attracts quite a lot of rain, and this rainwater feeds all of the numerous freshwater wells and springs on Nevis.

The mountain is home to a wide variety of interesting native birds, butterflies, wildflowers, and so on, and also serves as home to countless troops of Green Vervet monkeys, an introduced species which has flourished on Nevis for the last few hundred years. The monkeys tend to be shy of humans, but are very interested in the fruit that is grown in people's gardens, and in the numerous cultivated and half-wild Mango trees which are found all over the island.

It is possible to go on all kinds of interesting walks, hikes, and mountain-bike riding, on the less steep slopes of the mountain. Some of these walks are very pleasant and easy, but nonetheless they are interesting and rewarding, and will very much enrich your experience of Nevis.

For those who are interested in hiking (and climbing) all the way to the top of Nevis Peak, this is also a great adventure; it is however a challenging hike, for which a guide is recommended if you want to be sure you are safe. The trail involves some vertical sections with ropes, and it is not suitable for the faint-hearted. Several parts are slippery after it rains (it rains often on the peak). You need to be in good shape physically, and not averse to getting muddy! Lightweight hiking boots are definitely a good idea, and weight-lifting gloves are helpful to protect your hands when pulling yourself up or lowering yourself down the vertical sections using ropes and roots. Take plenty of water and a snack to eat at the top to give you energy for the climb down.

New River Estate

New River Estate is on the Atlantic or eastern side of Nevis (the Caribbean is the western side of the island.) This estate was still processing sugar commercially until 1958, when it finally closed down, the last sugar mill to operate on Nevis.

Many of the buildings of New River estate are still reasonably intact, at least compared with the much older ruins of plantation sugar mills and associated buildings which are readily visible in the landscape of Nevis, scattered all over the the island. In particular at New River there are the impressive remains of the huge steam engine (manufactured in 1883) which was used to crush the cane. This was a "modern' improvement on the older system of windpower from windmills.

Newcastle Beach

Newcastle Beach is on the northern side of Nevis, and so it faces the Narrows and the Atlantic Ocean rather than the Caribbean Sea.

The beach is named after the small village of Newcastle, which had to be moved out of the way when the Nevis airport runway was extended years ago in order to accomodate turboprop and jet planes. Most of Newcastle Beach is yellow sand, but one part (Herbert's Beach, now very small) has white coralline sand instead.

The beach reaches all the way from near the airport, to the south end of tiny Herberts Beach, which is south of Nisbet Plantation. Nisbet Plantation Resort really looks after their section of beach, and rakes it carefully every morning. They have a very nice beach bar, Sea Breeze, and a lovely beachfront restaurant, Coconuts, where breakfast is served next to the pool.

The palm trees of Nisbet reach down close to the water, which in this part of the island is a lagoon area behind a fringing coral reef. Most of the lagoon is turtle grass over coral rock, with sand in some places, but there is decent amount of sand between the breakwaters by the beach, and there is some good snorkeling offshore: the lagoon area is in fact a rich marine habitat, even though it may look rather 'plain' with a lot of turtle grass and very little coral except at the far rim.

Oualie Beach

Oualie was the original name of the island of Nevis. The word is pronounced "wah-lee" and means beautiful waters, referring not just to the Caribbean Sea and Atlantic Ocean, but to the many volcanic and freshwater springs on Nevis.

Oualie Bay (formerly known as Mosquito Bay) is attractively shaped, and extremely sheltered.

The sand is a very pretty pale yellow, and there are many different kinds of both water and land activities and sports available here.

The bay is home to the Oualie Beach Hotel. And it is also home to Scuba Safaris, Nevis Water Sports (fishing), and Windsurfing / Mountain Biking Nevis.

Oualie Bay has a dock, which means that water taxis can drop off passengers here, which is another convenience.

Pinney's Beach

Pinneys is a fine beach, the longest beach on Nevis. It is on the Caribbean side of the island, where the sea is usually quite calm.

This beach is almost 3 miles long, reaching from just outside of Charlestown all the way to the north end of Cades Bay. You can walk the whole length of the beach, including going past the lagoon at Nelson's Spring. And if you do walk the whole beach, you will only have to go off the sand a little way at two points, once because of a small rocky point, and the other time because of the rocks which were put down by the Four Seasons in 2005 to protect the north end of their property against erosion.

The sand on Pinney's Beach is a pleasant pale yellow-grey color. Parts of the beach are still relatively wild, and you will see usually see pelicans fishing as well as shy Night Herons resting. Sometimes there are shells washed up here and there on Pinney's, depending on what the sea has been doing recently. You will also see brightly-painted, hand-made fishing boats, pulled up on the beach just north of Four Seasons.

The southern half of Pinney's also has Turtle Beach Bar & Grill, Sunshine's beach bar and at the southern end, Double Deuce Beach Bar.

Sunshine's

Sunshine's is a popular beach bar, located on Pinney's Beach, a little way south of the Four Seasons Resort. They recently had to move further down the beach to just south of Chevy's.

They serve a rum punch known as the "Killer Bee", made to a secret recipe, and people also seem to really enjoy the lobster, although be warned, sometimes they do run out.

This beach bar has been a popular place on Nevis since the Four Season's Resort opened in 1991, and is both a local and celebrity hangout.

The Caves

This dive site is actually known as "Devil's Caves" and it is on the southwestern side of Nevis, just where the Caribbean Sea meets the Atlantic Ocean. It's a 35 minutes boat ride to get there, and the seas need to be relatively calm, otherwise it's not possible to dive at this location.

This location is a series of caves and overhangs which divers can swim through. Visible are lava spills, and the remains of a 17th century shipwreck and anchor. If you are lucky you might see a Black Tip Reef Shark. Huge numbers of of fish live in the area, including Snappers, Grunts,

Black-Durgeons and Squirrel-fish, as well as Chubb, Blue Tangs, and Glassy Sweepers. You will also probably see Nurse Sharks, Stingrays, and lobster.

At present there are numerous good dive sites around Nevis, but there is only one on-island dive operator.

Windward Beach

Windward Beach is a long, sand beach on the southeastern, or "windward", coast of Nevis.

Windward means facing into the Trade Winds, tropical winds which blow almost all the time, and which keep Nevis at a pleasant temperature.

On the Ordnance Survey map, Windward Beach is known as "White Bay" and the bluff (an ancient volcanic core of reddish rock) is known as "Red Cliff". Windward Beach is one of the best beaches on the Atlantic coast, and it has quite a different atmosphere from the beaches on the Caribbean side of Nevis. You get to this beach by following Hanley's Road to the end, and then head down the dirt roads, turning left towards the Racetrack, and just keep going, past the old stables. You have to park near the bluff where the dirt road peters out, and then walk down a short distance to get to the sand.

This is a wild beach, completely undeveloped, with no facilities, although Golden Rock Hotel does own a fairly large parcel of land here. It seems unlikely that you could board surf here, but maybe you could body surf sometimes. Either way the water can be fun to go out in, as long as you really do know how to swim, and are comfortable in waves.

Day Trips

From Nevis a day trip can take visitors to neighbouring Caribbean islands, such as St. Kitts (an easy ferry crossing), St. Bart's or St. Martin (charter or regular flights, or perhaps a private boat trip).

Visitors can also ask at the ticket booths in the ferry terminal at the port in Charlestown if any special ferry trips are planned; sometimes a trip to Montserrat or Sint Eustatius is available.

So it's certainly possible to spend time on other islands if you would like to, but a lot of people fall in love with Nevis itself and want to stay on and around the island for the whole of their vacation time.

Half- or full-day sailing charters can be arranged, on monohulls or catamarans. Deep sea fishing can fill up a morning, and then the afternoon can be used to relax after hauling in a big one. Then there are 3-4 hour kayaking trips, windsurfing, snorkelling with marine biologists, diving, and coastal boat historical tours. These are all for the aquatic-minded, but what about things for the landlubbers?

For a really muddy adventure in the West Indies, try going up Nevis Peak and back down again (4 to 6 hours, guide recommended) or take off Mountain Biking on the old Esate Roads. Too much like hard work? Numerous shorter, easier trails are available into historic ruins or the Rain Forest, as well as Island Taxi Tours.

This is what makes Nevis so pleasant: groups are always small and everybody can find something they really like!

Dining Scene

Some people who travel to the tropics wonder if it is going to be safe to eat salads, fresh fruits and vegetables, and to drink the water. None of this is a problem on Nevis. You are welcome to dine anywhere at all: the food will always be safe, and tasty too.

As far as dressing for dinner goes, whether you prefer to be semi-formally dressed, or casually dressed, both types of dining are available. Most of the hotel restaurants request long pants, shoes, and collared shirts for men, but Oualie Beach Hotel is a place for less formal attire, and yet it still has excellent food. Many places have a casual night, or can help you find a place where you will feel comfortable dressed down. In the smaller local places, t-shirts and tennis shoes are just fine.

Cost varies even more than attire. There are places where you can get $500 bottles of wine served by waiters in suits. In contrast there are, village eateries where you can get a pleasant, very inexpensive, and very informal meal,. These eateries are called 'Snackettes'; you will see signs for them often, when you drive around the island. At the Snackettes a full meal featuring local fish cakes or chicken costs only about $10, self-service. Both the very expensive and the very inexpensive places have certain advantages, depending on what you require: the more formal dining room might be nice for that romantic popping of the question, while the cheaper self-service places are very useful when you need to get the kids fed and out again reasonably quickly.

Which brings up a point about timing of food service. Service on Nevis can be quite slow (except for the snackettes of course.) This is because food is not usually prepared in advance; small places would not be able to stay in business if they cooked everything in advance and then hardly anyone came that night. So please do not expect the kind of rapid service that you might be used to back home in places that serve hundreds of customers a day with pre-prepared meals. Sit, relax, have a drink (or several drinks,) and anticipate the freshly-prepared meal. If you are really hungry, one nice thing is to have a cold soup or hot fritters to tide you over until the main course is ready. If on the other hand you are genuinely in a hurry, with small children who cannot wait, or perhaps if you are with impatient adults, please call the restaurant in advance, and put in your order over the phone; with sufficient notice most places will be able to have dinner waiting for you when you get there.

If you are interested in exploring the local culture, you can try some Nevis dishes that are are local Caribbean specialities, things you don't find in North America and Europe. For example, you will also come across fritters, made either from conch, or from tannia, a tropical root vegetable; these fritters are crispy delicacies with secret seasonings added. A delicious local mutton stew (called "goat water") varies a lot; sometimes it is spicy and sometimes not; some stews have dumplings and some don't; some places remove the bones, whereas some places feel that the bones add extra flavour. Nevis restaurants also make several very good cold soups that you will almost certainly enjoy.

Business Dining

Nevis is known throughout the Caribbean and the world for high-class finance. It has more lawyers and bankers per capita than just about anywhere else in the world, even Washington, D.C.! This means that there are lots of places for fine cuisine and business dining to help impress that special client.

For those wanting something formal, Montpelier has a wonderful Mill Tower set up that is very private with exceptional cuisine. There is also the fine dining room at Four Seasons, which can handle a bit larger crowd. Nisbet Plantaion will set up something special, and many deals are closed over lunch at Hermitage Hotel.

If you prefer something more casual, and not quite as private, check out Oualie Beach Hotel or Golden Rock; both have beautiful vistas and good food. Those wanting to party and celebrate can also try somewhere like Chevy's or Sunshine's.

Bananas

Bananas" is a first-class restaurant surrounded by a lovely tropical garden tucked in to the edge of the forest. It is not easy to find your way there, as it is up in the hills above Church Ground. The elevation means that the vegetation is much more lush and the air much breezier and cooler than down near the coast.

The food at Bananas is international with a Nevisian influence, and it is all very well thought out and beautifully prepared. The table settings are elegant and the service is pretty much flawless. If possible get to Bananas before the sun sets; that way you can watch the sunset in as you relax with a tropical drink.

Breakfast

This is the relaxed part of the Caribbean, and therefore hotel breakfasts on Nevis generally do not start earlier than 8 am. But on your special request many of the hotels will prepare a packed breakfast of fruits and breads; and so if you want to get out in the early morning, you can order this the day before and pick it up from the staff.

For people who feel they need a solid, sit-down breakfast quite early in the morning (this might be golfers, divers, or people who are going out on fishing expeditions) generally speaking, the two places on Nevis where you can reliably get breakfast served at a table before 8:00 am are Four Seasons Resort and Oualie Beach Hotel.

For people who like to get up and eat at the regular time, there are some excellent places to have breakfast around the island. Golden Rock Hotel starts serving round about 8:00, however, if you go up there a bit early and walk through the gardens and grounds, maybe you will be lucky enough to see some monkeys. Or you may want to try the excellent coconut French toast at Hermitage. Meals at Montpelier at any time are something special, and a thrasher (a handsome, large, thrush-like bird) sometimes will come over to entertain you. See how the sun lights up the nearby island of St. Kitts as you sit in the restaurant at Mount Nevis Hotel.

At Nisbet Plantation breakfast is served from 8 am to 10 am, very near the ocean. Each day they have one of several kinds of pancakes you can try: for example, with coconut or mango, and they also make almond-crusted French toast. A fresh-squeezed fruit juice of the day is always available, along with a very wide selection of fresh fruits. The occasional bananaquit (a pretty little black and yellow bird) may attempt to assist you with your fruit selection.

Local places? Try one of the bakeries in town for freshly baked buns or raisin rolls. Here in the West Indies people make some lovely breads.

Dining for Large Groups

Some places on Nevis offer dining for groups, but not every place on Nevis can easily accomodate a large number of people. If you are one of a large group (on this small Caribbean island, that means 6 people or more) and you are planning to go somewhere to eat, you should always call first so they can set up and reserve a nice arrangement of tables for you. If the group is big enough, they may actually allow you to take over the whole restaurant.

Really large groups of more than 50 should probably only use the hotels and the bigger more upscale restaurants. These localities have the staff and facilities to get the food ready in a reasonable time, and everybody can sit down together to eat. Four Seasons has Banquet Facilities for company functions and weddings; they can seat several hundred people. Other places that can seat larger groups, either indoors or outdoors, include Old Manor, Hermitage, Nisbet Plantation, Montpelier, Mount Nevis Hotel, Golden Rock, Oualie, or even Ms. June's. There is also Coconut Grove and Banana's which have lovely facilities and trained staff.

The Hermitage has a covered dining area for around 50, but can expand outside for parties.

Less formal places, which are also willing to work with groups, and which have even more of a 'party' atmosphere, include Chevy's Calypso Bar & Grill, Sunshines, V's Courtyard, Night Moves and Double Deuce. These are great places for outside parties, bonfires, and dancing!

Dining with a View

Many of the small restaurants on Nevis look out over the Caribbean Sea. In fact, excellent views of the beach and the water are very frequently encountered in Nevis eating places, and almost all the hotels also have beautiful views of the central mountain, Nevis Peak. That being said, here are suggestions for some places which have the best cuisine, as well as fine views.

Golden Rock Hotel, high up at 1,000 feet, serves excellent lobster sandwiches for lunch, and the scenic vista, overlooking the Atlantic Ocean with views of the islands of Redonda, Monserrat and Antigua in the distance, is unequaled. In the morning, sunrise is particularly lovely here, and there are often monkeys around.

There is also fine dining and fine views of St. Kitts at Mount Nevis Hotel, Oualie Beach Hotel and Nisbet Plantation. All these have outdoor tables and excellent cuisine. Garden dining can be truly wonderful at The Hermitage. Montpelier Plantation Inn offers dining out on the terrace with views of St. Kitts and the lights of Charlestown, as well as dining inside the Mill, which is an 18th century sugar mill with views of St. Kitts and other evening lights. Enjoy lunch oceanside at Nisbet Plantation's 'Sea Breeze' restaurant and dinner at the Great House (circa 1778) where you can gaze out over the elegant Avenue of Palms which leads down to the beach and the water.

Slightly less sophisticated, but with excellent views and very good local food and seafood are Chevy's Calypso Bar & Grill, Shirley's, and Double Deuce.

Late-night Dining

Most of the hotels on the island require reservations for dinner and they stop serving after 9:00 pm. (Nevis is a relaxing Caribbean destination, and part of the plan for rest and relaxation is that you can enjoy your beauty sleep.) So not everywhere serves dinner late, but two of the late night dining choices on Nevis are of course room service at The Four Seasons or going to the smaller local restaurants. (There are no drive-throughs or fast food places on the island.)

On Nevis there are several high-quality, authentic Chinese Restaurants operated by people from Hong Kong. A quick plate of Won Tons is a delicious possibility for late-night food.

The small, truly local eating places on Nevis are completely used to having people drop in for music or socializing, and they will usually be able to fix up something good for you to eat on short notice. Perhaps you could ask for fritters: they are fried and come with a dipping sauce. Chips (fries) are almost always available, and so is chicken. Ribs from the Water Department (only on Fridays) or Mansa's are easy to find, and are quite exceptional. Chevy's Calypso Bar & Grill (two minutes walk south of the Four Seasons

Resort) will always be able to make you a sandwich at the very least. Sunday's are Reggae Nights with live music from 5pm and Mondays are great fun till late at Chevy's with Dinner & Karaoke fun! Rumours is also good for a late night snack. Several of the local Rum Shops are open and sell fried fish and also chicken legs, you are safe and welcome there. (Have a drink while you are there as well as some food).

Nature's Way

If you are interested in some really delicious vegetarian food, "Nature's Way" is the place to go. This small and very unpretentious place is just outside Charlestown, not far from Rams supermarket, in Stoney Grove.

You can get your meal "to go" or you can sit down to eat. There are only three very small tables, and there is no "ambience" here, but the food is really superb, authentic Nevisian dishes, hearty, satisfying, and with wonderful seasonings. It is also extremely good value. Should you be interested for a special occasion, Nature's Way also does very good catering.

It is not possible to get an alcoholic drink here, but you may want to try the locally made ginger beer instead.

If you are able to cook while you are on Nevis, you may wish to buy yourself some health-food type groceries at the related "Myrtle's Healthy Beginnings", next door.

People-watching

Nevis, unlike many places in the Caribbean, doesn't really have many "trendy" spots, and so where the crowds are depends on what is happening that night. People looking for the rich and famous might try Sunshine's or hang around Pinney's Beach near The Four Seasons .

Quite a lot of movie stars, politicians, rock stars and singers come here, but please remember that, like you, they come to Nevis to relax and to be away from the crowds. They also get a lot of models (Victoria's Secret recently shot ads on Nevis) and sports teams also sometimes come down to the West Indies for a nice vacation. Feel free to say hi, but please don't pester them, as most of them are just hoping to relax and enjoy themselves like "normal people" for a while.

Where do these celebrities hang out? All over. They can be up the mountainside hiking, down on the beach, or having lunch on the patio at Golden Rock. They may be at Karaoke Night at either Eddy's or Chevy's. One may be sitting next to you on your sailing and snorkeling trip. They are on vacation just like you are, and hopefully they are having as much fun as you are!

But you can certainly also watch local people. "Jam Man" sings and dances as he wanders around the island picking up trash. Some of the bartenders can be quite entertaining. Or perhaps you would like to meet a few of the local fishermen when they pull in their boats after their early morning fishing trip. They sell their catch at the top of the beach just down the road from the courthouse in Charlestown. You will enjoy seeing the fishermen's brightly-painted, hand-made boats and the amazing variety of colorful fish they sell, as well as meeting the fishermen themselves.

It's also interesting to just sit in one of Charlestown's two main squares, especially on market days, and watch people come and go, that way you get a bit of a sense of what life is really like on Nevis.

Riviere House Restaurant

Riviere House Restaurant is a relatively recent addition to Nevis dining. The food is really excellent and the prices are very reasonable. The ambiance is elegant and the staff are friendly.

Located in Charlestown on Government Road, a 100-year-old Nevisian house has been converted into a very elegant and attractive restaurant with a really large and cool covered porch at the back. There are numerous pieces of art and jewelry exhibited indoors which can be purchased if you are so inclined. The profits from the jewelry and art sales go to support several local charities, primarily the Nevis Hospital.

Riviere House is open Tuesdays through Saturdays for both lunch and dinner, plus they have special events throughout the year. Prices are in Eastern Caribbean dollars and are less expensive than many other places, yet with exceptional quality food. Well worth a visit when on Nevis.

The Cafe des Arts.

A very popular, cheerful, relaxed-style restaurant in Charlestown is "Cafe des Arts". It is located right next to the Alexander Hamilton Museum. A stone wall encloses a large courtyard area with various decorative plants and a few small trees, as well as (often) a few chickens and a rooster wandering about.

Cafe des Arts is unusual in that both tourists and locals enjoy eating there, which makes it good for people-watching. The Cafe serves breakfast, lunch and dinner, and has sandwiches, burgers, fries, as well as a few more interesting dishes.

Riviere House Restaurant

Riviere House Restaurant is a relatively recent addition to Nevis dining. The food is really excellent and the prices are very reasonable. The ambiance is elegant and the staff are friendly.

Located in Charlestown on Government Road, a 100-year-old Nevisian house has been converted into a very elegant and attractive restaurant with a really large and cool covered porch at the back. There are numerous pieces of art and jewelry exhibited indoors which can be purchased if you are so inclined. The profits from the jewelry and art sales go to support several local charities, primarily the Nevis Hospital.

Riviere House is open Tuesdays through Saturdays for both lunch and dinner, plus they have special events throughout the year. Prices are in Eastern Caribbean dollars and are less expensive than many other places, yet with exceptional quality food. Well worth a visit when on Nevis.

Cheap Eats

Nevis is a good place to come to get away from mass-produced fast food, because it is one Caribbean island that is mercifully free of Burger King, McDonalds and Subway Sandwich shops. Instead there are a wide variety of very good inexpensive places to get freshly prepared food, including local dishes.

Your best choice for "Cheap Eats" on Nevis is to try one of the very good roadside vendors, such as the Yellow Bus in Charlestown, or the Water Department on Pump Road (great ribs and a good local spot on Friday nights).

There is also Mansa's at Cades Bay, which sells freshly-barbequed ribs and chicken, and has ice cream available in a freezer, as well as being a very good farmstand with all kinds of really excellent fruit and vegetables, not to mention lovely juices, sarsaparilla, and ginger beer freshly made at the farm.

Several bakeries and local shops, for example (Deli by Wendy) offer homemade breads, sandwiches, rotis and saltfish cakes. Here you could maybe pick up something to snack on at the beach (but please don't leave litter).

The smaller local restaurants such as Chevy's Calypso Bar & Grill located on Pinney's Beach serve great local food, international food and seafood, and are much less expensive that the hotels. You can also try dining at Rumours, Pemo's, Shirley's, and Callabahoo. Several of these also have lovely places to sit while you eat.

Family-friendly Dining

On Nevis, most places have either booster seats or high chairs, but kid's menus as such are not commonly found in the Caribbean. Some eating places are more adult-oriented in their cuisine, but they still welcome families. Four Seasons is one place which does have a Kid's Menu, and they will give out crayons and entertain the children too. Most other places simply give kid's discounts and children's plates if you request that.

Good places for children include most of the smaller restaurants such as Chevy's Calypso Bar (the kids can run, make noise, and no one cares). Oualie Beach Resort (the kids can go outside and chase the crabs along the shore) has very child-friendly staff and very child-friendly food too! Golden Rock also has sandwiches and fries; their beach pavilion is near to Sunshine's and the Four Seasons, while the Golden Rock hotel restaurant itself is up on the mountainside. Children are safe in any eating place on Nevis.

Outdoor Dining

Outdoor dining is a wonderful choice in the Caribbean; Nevis is no exception and the cuisine is second to none. On Nevis, unlike many other places in the West Indies and the tropics in general, mosquitos are not usually much of a problem. The breezes and late night showers also make everything cool and fresh, and there are some lovely garden spots.

Where to go? Hotels that offer outside dining with beautiful vistas from decks, patios or terraces include just about every hotel on Nevis: Four Seasons, Golden Rock, Hermitage Hotel, Montpelier, Mount Nevis, Nisbet Plantation, Old Manor, and Oualie. Each one has its own different appeal, and all are good for breakfast, lunch, or dinner.

You can also try ordering a picnic lunch from your hotel and then hike to eat your sandwiches up in the rain forest, or out on one of Nevis' more secluded beaches. But please do remember to take your litter away afterwards; Nevis residents are proud of their beautiful green island, and try as best as they can to prevent litter from being a problem.

Special Occasion Dining

For special occasion dining, you might want to give most of the small local Caribbean restaurants a miss, and stick to the fine dining at the hotels. Local places tend to be very busy, and so they can be a bit loud, with lots of children, and this is not usually what one wants for a romantic or formal dining experience.

Three of the best elegant places would be Montpelier Plantation, Hermitage Hotel, and Nisbet Plantation. Montpelier can put you in the Mill Tower which is very elegant. Hermitage and Nisbet will find you a lovely secluded spot for a private dinner. The cuisine at all of these places is excellent.

Celebrations are usually a bit noisier, but again, if speeches are in the forecast, it would be a good idea to avoid the small local places. You might want to try Oualie Beach Hotel or Four Seasons. They do very well with groups, have excellent menus and good service. Their dining rooms can accomodate various size groups. Montpelier also has space for small private functions, or it is possible for the bride and groom to take over the hotel for their special event.

Other fine dining establishments which are not part of hotels include Bananas and Coconut Grove.

The End

Made in United States
North Haven, CT
07 February 2022

15835386R00108